Communism and its Collapse

The Russian Revolution of 1917 was a turning point in the twentieth century. The revolutions that swept through the USSR and Eastern Europe at the end of the 1980s marked another turning point. *Communism and its Collapse* surveys the course of communism and addresses the many intriguing questions that the experience of communism has generated.

Focusing particularly on the USSR and Eastern Europe, this book examines the development of communist rule in historical and analytical terms and includes discussion of:

* communism as a doctrine
* the evolution of communist rule
* the challenges to Soviet authority that came from Yugoslavia and Hungary, and how communism worked in Czechoslovakia and Poland
* the complex processes bringing an end to communist rule in the 1980s
* rival historiographical interpretations of the whole mechanism of change.

Communism and its Collapse is an essential introduction to the study of this crucial element of twentieth-century history.

Stephen White is Professor of Politics at the University of Glasgow. His many published works include *The Bolshevik Poster* (Yale, 1988), *After Gorbachev* (Cambridge, 1994), *Russia's New Politics* (Cambridge, 2000) and, with Evan Mawdsley, *The Soviet Elite from Lenin to Gorbachev* (Oxford, 2000).

The Making of the Contemporary World
Edited by Eric Evans and Ruth Henig
University of Lancaster

The Making of the Contemporary World series provides challenging interpretations of contemporary issues and debates within strongly defined historical frameworks. The range of the series is global, with each volume drawing together material from a range of disciplines – including economics, politics and sociology. The books in this series present compact, indispensable introductions for students studying the modern world.

Titles include:

The Uniting of Europe
From Discord to Concord
Stanley Henig

International Economy since 1945
Sidney Pollard

**United Nations in the
Contemporary World**
David Whittaker

Latin America
John Ward

Thatcher and Thatcherism
Eric J. Evans

Decolonization
Raymond F. Betts

China Under Communism
Alan Lawrance

The Cold War
An Interdisciplinary History
David Painter

Forthcoming titles:

Multinationals
Peter Wardley

Pacific Asia
Yumei Zhang

Conflicts in the Middle East since 1945
Beverley Milton-Edwards and Peter Hinchcliffe

The Irish Question
Patrick Maume

Right Wing Extremism
Paul Hainsworth

The Soviet Union in World Politics:
Coexistence, Revolution and Cold War
1945–1991
Geoffrey Roberts

US Foreign Policy Since 1945
Alan Dobson and Steve Marsh

Dividing and Uniting Germany
J.K.A. Thomianeck and Bill Niven

**Women and Political Power in Europe
since 1945**
Ruth Henig and Simon Henig

States and Nationalism
Malcolm Anderson

Communism and its Collapse

Stephen White

Routledge
Taylor & Francis Group

LONDON AND NEW YORK

First published 2001
by Routledge
2 Park Square, Milton Park, Abingdon, Oxon OX14 4RN

Simultaneously published in the USA and Canada
by Routledge
270 Madison Ave, New York NY 10016

Transferred to Digital Printing 2009

Routledge is an imprint of the Taylor & Francis Group, an informa business

Reprinted 2003

Typeset in Times by Keystroke, Jacaranda Lodge, Wolverhampton
Printed and bound in Great Britain by TJI Digital, Padstow,
Cornwall

British Library Cataloguing in Publication Data
A catalogue record for this book is available from the British Library

Library of Congress Cataloging in Publication Data
White, Stephen, 1945–
    Communism and its collapse / Stephen White.
    p. cm. — (The making of the contemporary world)
    Includes bibliographical references and index.
    1. Communism—Soviet Union—History. 2. Communism—
    Europe, Eastern—History. 3. Soviet Union—Politics and
    government—1985–1991. 4. Soviet Union—History—1985–1991.
    5. Europe, Eastern—Politics and government—1989– 6. Europe,
    Eastern—History—1989– I. Title. II. Series.
HX44 .W444 2000
335.43—dc21   00–042186

ISBN 10: 0-415-24423-4 (hbk)
ISBN 10: 0-415-17180-6 (pbk)

ISBN 13: 978-0-415-24423-7 (hbk)
ISBN 13: 978-0-415-17180-9 (pbk)

Contents

Chronology

1917	Nov	Bolshevik revolution in Russia
1919–20		Paris Peace Settlement
1924	Jan	Death of Lenin
1928	Oct	First Soviet Five-Year Plan
1929	Jan	Trotsky expelled from USSR
1935	July–Aug	'Popular Front' strategy adopted by 7th Comintern Congress
1939	Aug	Nazi–Soviet Pact
	Sep	Start of Second World War
1941	June	German invasion of the Soviet Union
1943	Jan	German army at Stalingrad surrenders
	May	Dissolution of Comintern
1943–4		Red Army reconquers German-occupied Soviet Union
1944–5		Red Army liberates most of Eastern Europe
1945	Feb	Yalta Conference
	May	Red Army enters Berlin
	July–Aug	Potsdam Conference
1946	Mar	Churchill's 'Iron Curtain' speech
1947	Mar	Truman Doctrine espoused
	June	Marshall Plan
	Sep	Cominform established
1948	Feb	Communist coup in Czechoslovakia Start of Stalin–Tito dispute
	June	Yugoslavia expelled from Cominform; Berlin Blockade starts
1948–52		Titoist purges across Eastern Europe
1949	Jan	Comecon established
	Apr	NATO established
	Oct	Chinese People's Republic proclaimed
1950–3		Korean War

1953	Mar	Death of Stalin
	June	Demonstrations in East Berlin suppressed
1955	Feb	Khrushchev replaces Malenkov as Soviet premier
	May	Warsaw Pact established; Soviet withdrawal from Austria
	June	Khrushchev–Tito declaration of reconciliation
1956	Feb	Khrushchev denounces Stalin in 'secret speech' at 20th Congress of Communist Party of Soviet Union
	Apr	Cominform disbanded
	Oct	'Polish October' headed by Gomułka
	Nov	Hungarian uprising suppressed by Red Army
1957	June	Khrushchev purges 'Anti-Party Group' opposed to his leadership
1959	Jan	Fidel Castro's 26 July Movement comes to power in Cuba
1960	July–Aug	Soviet technicians withdrawn from China; emergence of Sino-Soviet dispute
1961	Aug	Construction of Berlin Wall
	Oct	22nd Soviet Communist Congress initiates new de-Stalinisation
1962	Oct	Cuban Missile Crisis
1964	Oct	Khrushchev replaced by Brezhnev as Soviet party leader
1965	Mar	Ceauşescu new leader of Romania
1966	Aug	'14 Points' launch Chinese Cultural Revolution
1968	Jan	Dubček replaces Novotny as Czechoslovak party leader; start of 'Prague Spring'
	Aug	Warsaw Pact invasion and occupation of Czechoslovakia
	Nov	'Brezhnev Doctrine' announced; 'normalisation' imposed upon Czechoslovakia
1970	Dec	Riots in Poland
1971	Feb	Gierek replaces Gomułka as Polish party leader
1975	Apr	North Vietnamese and Vietcong forces enter Saigon
1976	June	Strikes in Poland force government to withdraw price increase
	Sep	Death of Mao Zedong and arrest of 'Gang of Four'
1977	Jan	Charter 77 founded in Czechoslovakia
	Oct	New 'Brezhnev Constitution' in Soviet Union
1978	Oct	Cardinal Wojtyła elected first Polish Pope
	Dec	Soviet invasion of Afghanistan
1980	July–Aug	Strikes in Poland; formation of Solidarity
1981	Dec	Martial law imposed in Poland
1982	Nov	Death of Brezhnev, succeeded by Andropov
1984	Feb	Death of Andropov, succeeded by Chernenko
1985	Mar	Death of Chernenko, succeeded by Gorbachev

1986	Apr	Chernobyl nuclear accident
1987	Jan	CPSU Central Committee approves 'democratisation'
1988	Mar	Start of Soviet withdrawal from Afghanistan
	Aug	Strikes force Polish government to negotiate with Solidarity
1989	May	Hungary dismantles its Iron Curtain
	June	Solidarity landslide in Polish general election; Tiananmen Square massacre in China
	Aug	Solidarity-led government appointed in Poland
	Sep	Hungary permits exodus of East Germans to West
	Nov	Breaching of Berlin Wall; fall of Zhivkov in Bulgaria
	Nov–Dec	'Velvet Revolution' in Czechoslovakia
	Dec	'Christmas Revolution' in Romania removes Ceauşescu
1990	Feb	CPSU Central Committee renounces party's claim to a political monopoly in Article 6 of Constitution
	Mar	Lithuania declares independence
	May	Yeltsin elected Chairman of Russian Parliament
	Oct	Germany formally reunified
1991	Mar	Referendum on future of Soviet Union
	Apr	Novo-Ogarevo Accord on new USSR federal treaty
	June	Comecon formally dissolved; Yeltsin elected President of Russia
	July	Warsaw Pact formally dissolved
	Aug	Attempted coup in Moscow to stop new Union Treaty; Soviet Communist Party suppressed
	Dec	Ukraine declares independence from Soviet Union; formation of Commonwealth of Independent States, initially by Russia, Ukraine and Belarus; Gorbachev resigns; Soviet Union dissolved

1   What was communism?

Karl Marx told workers they 'had no country': in other words, they had a common interest more important than the national loyalties that might otherwise have divided them. In 1917 the world's first socialist state was established in the USSR on the basis of his teachings. And for more than seventy years, latterly in association with a group of states in Eastern Europe and Asia, it was governed on the basis of Marx's belief that human labour was the only source of wealth, that productive resources should be owned by the people as a whole, and that the working class in capitalist as well as socialist countries would recognise their common interest in a form of shared ownership that would eventually extend across state boundaries. It was the longest attempt that has so far been made to place 'an ideology in power'. What, in broad terms, was this ideology? And what role did it perform in the states that were committed to it?

COMMUNISM IN POWER

Until the late 1980s the USSR and the countries of Eastern Europe were ruled by communist parties formally dedicated to Marxism–Leninism. Together, they were known as the 'socialist community', and they formed a part of a wider group of communist-ruled countries that was officially known as the 'world socialist system' (see Table 1.1). The largest and longest-established of these states was the Union of Soviet Socialist Republics (USSR). Like its counterparts elsewhere, all aspects of public life in the USSR were dominated by a ruling party; and, as elsewhere, it was a single party that was committed to the establishment of a fully communist society. Under its constitution, the USSR's highest goal was the 'building of a classless communist society'; its political system was a 'socialist all-people's state'; its economic system was based on socialist ownership of the means of production of a kind that could not be used for personal gain or 'other selfish ends'. Equally, although articles of everyday use and even a house could be privately owned, no form of

Table 1.1 The communist states in the 1980s

Country	Date established	Area (thousand sq. km)	Population (million, 1987)	Level of development
Union of Soviet Socialist Republics	1917	22,402	283	(non-market economy)
Mongolian People's Republic	1924	1,565	2	lower middle-income
Albanian People's Republic	1944	29	3	(non-market economy)
Socialist Federal Republic of Yugoslavia	1945	256	23	upper middle-income
Socialist Republic of Vietnam	1945/76	330	65	low income
People's Republic of Bulgaria	1946	111	9	(non-market economy)
Socialist Republic of Romania	1947	238	23	upper middle-income
Polish People's Republic	1947	313	38	lower middle-income
Korean People's Democratic Republic	1948	121	21	lower middle-income
Czechoslovak Socialist Republic	1948	128	16	(non-market economy)
Hungarian People's Republic	1949	93	11	upper middle-income
German Democratic Republic	1949	108	17	(non-market economy)
Chinese People's Republic	1949	9,561	1069	low income
Republic of Cuba	1959	115	10	lower middle-income
Laotian People's Democratic Republic	1975	237	4	low income
People's Republic of Kampuchea	1975	181	7	low income

Note: Levels of development and population are as reported in the *World Development Report 1989* (New York: World Bank, 1989).

property could be used to derive unearned income or in a way that was detrimental to the wider society.

The Soviet authorities did not define the country over which they ruled as a 'communist society'. Communism, in their view, was a state of affairs that would be achieved at an unspecified point in the future, when the development of productive forces made the distribution of goods to all in accordance with their needs a real possibility, when communist, collectivist values had been accepted by the population at large. Until that point was reached, the USSR and its East European allies were held to be more properly described as 'socialist' societies. In societies of this kind the means of production (factories, farms and so forth) had been taken into public ownership, and there was no longer a capitalist class that made a living from employing – or, in the official view, 'exploiting' – others. Equally, however, the state still existed (as it was not supposed to do under communism) and the distribution of rewards was determined by the work that people did, rather than by their needs. Only when the higher stage of communism had been reached would the state disappear and distribution be determined by people's needs rather than by the work they performed.

In the Soviet case the single most authoritative statement of the official ideology was the Programme of the Communist Party of the Soviet Union, a new and revised version of which was adopted by the 27th Party Congress in 1986. This defined communism in the following terms:

> Communism is a classless social system with one form of public own-ership of the means of production and with full social equality of all members of society. Under communism, the all-round development of people will be accompanied by the growth of productive forces on the basis of continuous progress in science and technology, all the springs of social wealth will flow abundantly, and the great principle, 'from each according to his ability, to each according to his needs', will be imple-mented. Communism is a highly organised society of free, socially conscious working people, a society in which public self-government will be established, a society in which labour for the good of society will become the prime vital requirement of everyone, a clearly recognised necessity, and the ability of each person will be employed to the greatest benefit of the people.

The achievement of a communist society of this kind was described in the Programme as the CPSU's 'ultimate goal'; the much more general transi-tion from capitalism to socialism and communism on a worldwide scale was described, despite its 'unevenness, complexity and contradictoriness', as 'inevitable'.

The 1986 Programme replaced a more ambitious set of objectives that had been approved in 1961 under party leader Nikita Khrushchev. This, the third of the programmes that the USSR's ruling party had adopted since its foundation, was best known for its promise that a communist society would be established within twenty years. The construction of communism, the 1961 Programme promised, would be carried out in a series of stages. During the 1960s, the world's richest and most powerful capitalist country, the USA, would be overtaken in per capita production, hard physical labour would disappear, the Soviet people would all live in 'easy circumstances' and the USSR would have the shortest working day in the world. By the end of the 1970s, the Programme declared, an 'abundance of material and cultural values for the whole population' would have been created, a single form of property – public ownership – would predominate, and the principle of distribution according to people's needs would be close to attainment. By the end of the 1970s, the Programme went on to promise, a communist society would 'in the main' have been constructed in the USSR, to be 'fully completed' in the subsequent period. The Programme concluded with the words: 'The party solemnly proclaims: the present generation of Soviet people shall live in communism!'

Not simply was this Programme not fulfilled; it soon became impossible to refer to it in public, and no more was heard of the dates by which its ambitious targets were to be achieved. Leonid Brezhnev (Khrushchev's successor as party leader in 1964) introduced the rather different concept of 'developed socialism', which was a stage of socialism that would last for many years before a transition to communism could be contemplated. Brezhnev's successors Yuri Andropov and Konstantin Chernenko (party leaders from 1982 to 1984 and from 1984 to 1985, respectively) made it clear in turn that the Soviet Union was 'only at the beginning' of the stage of developed socialism, and called for more attention to be given to immediate and practical tasks rather than what Lenin had called the 'distant, beautiful and rosy future'. The Programme became increasingly out of line with these more realistic objectives, and in 1981 it was decided to redraft it. The drafting commission, chaired by Mikhail Gorbachev after his accession to the party leadership in the spring of 1985, brought this new version to the 27th Party Congress a year later. Officially it was just a revision of the 1961 Programme, but many, Gorbachev told the Congress, had suggested it should be considered an entirely new, fourth Programme because the changes it contained were so far-reaching.

The 1961 Programme, for instance, described itself as a 'programme for the building of a communist society'; the 1986 version talked only about the 'planned and all-round perfection of socialism' with a view to a 'further advance to communism through the country's accelerated socio-economic development'. In 1961 it was assumed that socialism alone could abolish exploitation, economic crisis and poverty; the 1986 revision claimed only that socialism offered 'advantages' and that it was a superior form of society to capitalism. No dates or stages were given through which the transition to communism was to proceed (forecasts of this kind were 'harmful'); and there were no references, as in the 1961 Programme, to the increasing provision of free public services, a guaranteed one-month paid holiday for all, or the withering away of the state – a classic Marxist goal (some had always maintained that the only thing that would ever wither away was the *idea* that the state should wither away). Indeed, there were few references to 'communism' of any kind in the new Programme; much more emphasis was placed upon eliminating defects in contemporary Soviet society such as profiteering, parasitism and careerism.

The new Programme presented an analysis of both domestic and international affairs. On the domestic front, the Programme put forward what it described as a plan for 'social progress' leading ultimately to the establishment of a fully communist society. The Bolshevik revolution of 1917 was held to have been a 'landmark in world history' that determined the main trends of development worldwide and launched the 'irreversible process of the replacement of capitalism by the new, communist socio-economic formation'. The basic means of production had passed into popular ownership, industrialisation and collectivisation had transformed the economy, and a 'cultural revolution' had taken place that had led to the 'development of creative forces and the intellectual flowering of the working man'. By the end of the 1930s a socialist form of society was held to have been 'essentially built' in the USSR, which had been fully and finally established after the defeat of Nazi Germany in the Second World War. A new stage began in the 1960s, when the USSR officially became a 'developed socialist society'.

In a society of this kind, productive resources were owned by the people as a whole and there was rapid economic and technological advance. There were equal rights to work and pay, and a wide range of social benefits was available without regard to income. There was equality between the different social groups, between men and women, and between the nationalities, and there was 'genuine democracy – power exercised for the people and by the people' based upon the broadest possible participation of ordinary citizens. More generally, a 'socialist way of life' was supposed to have come into existence on the basis of the principles of 'social justice, collectivism and comradely mutual assistance'. Further advances towards communism would take place (the Programme explained) as the economy became increasingly able to satisfy all reasonable needs and as the 'truly humanistic Marxist-Leninist ideology' became dominant. Internationally, at the same time, increasing numbers of countries were believed to be associating themselves with socialist principles as the 'general crisis of capitalism' continued to deepen.

TOWARDS A COMMUNIST SOCIETY

Clearly, if a fully communist society was to be achieved, there would have to be a series of related changes. First and most obviously, there would have to be an improvement in living standards so that all members of the society would be able to satisfy their reasonable requirements. But no less importantly, there would have to be a change in popular attitudes and values. Working people, for instance, even in a society that was based on public ownership, could still be affected by the 'private property mentality', and this might lead them to place their personal interests above those of the society as a whole or even to engage in black-market speculation and other anti-social activities. There was also the problem of nationalism. A fully communist society was supposed to be an internationalist one; that meant there could be no room for ways of thinking that divided working people from each other, to the advantage of their class opponents. A fully communist society was also supposed to be an atheist one, free of the 'superstition' that working people would find their ultimate fulfilment in a higher world and that the tasks of the current Five-Year Plan were not necessarily of greater importance.

For such reasons, the Soviet authorities and their counterparts in the other communist-ruled countries were committed from the outset to the development of a 'new man', one whose values and way of life would be appropriate to a future society in which there would no longer be class divisions. The Communist Party of the Soviet Union set out the characteristics of a new man of this kind in a 'moral code of the builder of communism' that was added to the party rules in 1961 at the same time as the new Programme was approved. The 'builder of communism', according to this statement, would be devoted to the communist cause, to the socialist motherland and to the other socialist countries. The builder of communism would also be committed to conscientious labour for the good of society (paraphrasing the Bible, the Programme made clear that 'he who does not work, neither shall he eat'). The builder of communism would have a high sense of public duty, honesty and truthfulness; he or she would have an uncompromising attitude to injustice, parasitism and money-grubbing, and would at the same time have a fraternal attitude to the working people of other countries.

Every effort was made to ensure that these values were extended to the whole society. This was reflected, first of all, in a system of formal political instruction, intended primarily but not exclusively for party members. There were three main levels: at the primary level the subjects of study included the biography of Lenin and current party policy; at advanced levels there was more emphasis upon party history, economics and philosophy. By the late 1970s more than 20 million people were enrolled at the various levels of this system, and more than 30 million were enrolled in a parallel system of economic education. Beyond this there was a system of 'mass-political work', based on a network of more than 5 million agitators or lecturers who visited workplaces and residential areas all over the country to explain various aspects of party policy; and a further system of 'visual agitation', including the posters and slogans that decorated factories and other public places. Particular attention was devoted to anniversaries, such as 22 April (Lenin's birthday), 1 May (May Day) and 7 November (the anniversary of the revolution itself); and there were campaigns on particular occasions, such as in the summer of 1977 when a new constitution was under discussion. Altogether, Brezhnev told the Soviet parliament, more than four-fifths of the entire adult population had taken at least a nominal part in the debate.

A special degree of attention was given to the rising generation. Schoolchildren were enrolled at the age of 7 in the Little Octobrists and then, at the age of 10, in the Pioneers. Finally, between the ages of 14 and 28, they could join the Komsomol or Young Communist League, the party's 'active assistant and reserve', which enrolled about half the young people within the relevant age-group and helped to 'educate [them] in the communist spirit'. The Pioneers, for instance, held meetings with veterans of the Second World War, and Old Bolsheviks; and they made regular visits to places of revolutionary significance, such as the cruiser *Aurora* in Leningrad that had fired the shots over the Winter Palace that had precipitated the revolutionary events of 1917. The education system itself made a further contribution. Party orthodoxy, for a start, was directly reflected in subjects such as history and geography, there were separate classes in civics that incorporated a simplified version of the official ideology, and the whole organisation of school life was designed to reinforce collective and cooperative forms of activity.

Still more important were the mass media, especially newspapers and television. A newspaper, Lenin had explained, was supposed to 'educate, agitate and organise', and all forms of the media came under the direct control of one of the departments of the party's central apparatus. Editors were approved by party committees, and given weekly briefings about the themes they should (or should not) cover. Newspapers and other publications were subject to a close and detailed censorship, established on a 'temporary' basis just after the revolution and in existence throughout the vast majority of the Soviet period. The censor's decisions were not made public (indeed, there could be no public reference to the existence of the censorship system itself), and they were not open to challenge. Television developed a national presence rather later, but by the end of the 1970s it was available to more than 86 per cent of the population; and it too reflected official priorities, with a strong emphasis upon the economic achievements of the communist world balanced by accounts of the deepening crisis of the capitalist countries.

The creative arts were also expected to perform an ideological purpose. Painting, for instance, was expected to be representational rather than abstract or allegorical; music was expected to have a recognisable tune; and novels were supposed to be optimistic in character, set ideally in a factory with an identifiable hero who should triumph in the end over the stubborn resistance of the class enemy. All of the arts were subject to the doctrine of 'socialist realism', first approved in 1934, in terms of which the 'truthful, historically concrete presentation of reality in its revolutionary development' had to be combined with the 'ideological remaking and education of toilers in the spirit of socialism'. Soviet writers who satisfied these requirements, like Mikhail Sholokhov, were published in large editions and became extremely rich. Those who did not, like Alexander Solzhenitsyn, were prevented from publishing their work and could even be forced into emigration. And foreign writers openly hostile to communism, such as George Orwell, could only be read with special permission (their books, and those of political oppositionists like Trotsky, were kept in the reserve stacks of Soviet libraries and did not normally appear in their catalogues).

This, then, was an extraordinarily detailed and comprehensive system of political persuasion. And, for some, it had been an extraordinarily effective system. The Soviet authorities, certainly, felt able themselves to claim by the 1970s that a 'new historic community of peoples' had come into being who shared a 'unity of economic, sociopolitical and cultural life, Marxist-Leninist ideology, and the interests and communist ideals of the working class'. There was, in fact, an increasing body of evidence that the campaign of mass persuasion had been less successful than party leaders had expected. Political lectures, it emerged, were often superficial and repetitive, they were attended unwillingly, and they tended to attract those who were already the best-informed and most committed – 'informing the informed and agitating the agitated', as a party journal put it. Relatively few, it appeared, gave any attention to the posters that decorated the street corners. Where they could, in the Baltic or East Germany, ordinary people turned to foreign radio or television, or to rumour and gossip, rather than the official media. And few read the editorial on the front page, which set out the party line.

Indeed, there were few signs, by the late 1970s and 1980s, that the communist society of the future was gradually emerging. There were far more religious believers, in spite of two generations of atheist propaganda, than members of the Communist Party. Young people, who held the key to the future, were becoming fascinated by Western pop culture. There was a flourishing black market. Crime was increasing in parallel, although the figures were not made available until the late 1980s. And ordinary workers were more interested in the bottle than in the fulfilment of the Five-Year Plan. Nor had there been much success with nationalism. It had supposedly been 'resolved in principle'; but by the late 1980s there were open conflicts in several parts of the USSR, with the Baltic republics pushing for independence and a violent clash between Armenians and Azerbaijanis over the disputed enclave of Nagorno-Karabakh (see Chapter 8). Internationally, the world socialist system was resisting further integration, and communist parties in the wider world were losing much of the political influence they had once commanded.

The establishment of communist rule was none the less the central development in twentieth-century politics; and for more than two generations it defined a group of states that owed their origin to the October revolution and subscribed to its ideal of a society that would give working people the full fruits of their labour. Looking back, it is easy to see the dangers implicit in a form of rule that gave power to a small minority so that they could emancipate others. Not simply was there a danger that they might begin to enjoy the benefits of office for themselves (it was Trotsky who had pointed out that 'he who has something to distribute never forgets himself'). There was also the danger that they might abuse the office they held, and that they might take for granted the support of ordinary people without allowing them an opportunity to hold their rulers to account through the ballot box, the courts of law and the mass media. It was the nineteenth-century anarchist Mikhail Bakunin who had pointed out to Marx that the state was more than an administrative framework: it was ultimately a group of people who might have an interest of their own that they would do their best to defend even if this was at odds with the interests of the wider society.

But if historical experience has shown the force of Bakunin's insight, it also suggested other features of communist rule and ones that help us to understand why it was a pole of attraction for millions of people inside and outside the countries in which it prevailed. The experience of communist rule suggested that an economy could grow rapidly, and that it could be harnessed to social purposes. It suggested that unemployment could be abolished, and that social inequalities could be limited and eventually eliminated. It suggested that illiteracy could be overcome, that women could be given the same rights as men, and that all could have access to health care and a dignified old age. Some of these, indeed, were ideals that had as much influence in the West as in the countries that were nominally committed to them. Reflecting on these questions in the late 1980s, Gorbachev thought the Russian revolution, in the end, might be seen in much the same way as the

French revolution had come to be regarded. It was the French revolution that had given the world its modern concepts of democracy and citizenship; but it was the Russian revolution that had underlined the importance of social justice and equality. Eighty years or more after the establishment of communist rule, it may be too soon to conclude that the issues it placed on the global agenda have been satisfactorily resolved even if the states that attempted to resolve them have mostly passed into history.

2 The establishment of communist rule

The Russian revolution of November 1917 had been carried through on the assumption that Russia, although a backward country and not 'ready' for revolution in the Marxist sense, could be used to break the economic links that held together the major capitalist powers and thus to bring about a European and eventually a worldwide communist revolution. At the time these perspectives did not seem entirely unrealistic. Immediately after the First World War ended, in 1918–19, there were revolutionary uprisings in many parts of the world, and in Europe Soviet republics were established in Bavaria and Hungary. In 1920 factories were occupied in Italy, and Councils of Action were set up in Great Britain to oppose government policy towards Russia. The following year there was a communist-led rising in central Germany, and in 1923 there were more serious attempts at insurrection in northern Germany and Bulgaria. In 1926 there was a general strike in Britain, and by about the same time a powerful communist presence had begun to establish itself in China and elsewhere in the colonial world.

Soviet influence over this developing movement was exercised through the Communist International, founded in 1919, which was based in Moscow and whose executive committee was dominated by Russians. The Comintern, as it was known, saw its task as the provision of revolutionary leadership for the workers and peasants of the developed and colonial countries; these were only held back from more decisive action, it was believed, by the caution of their reformist leaders. The Comintern's first congress issued a manifesto to the 'proletarians of the entire world' which called upon them to support the soviet form of government and the dictatorship of the proletariat. Its second congress, held in the summer of 1920, took place at a time when the Red Army was advancing into Poland and the entire postwar settlement appeared to be in the balance. Writing in the first issue of the Comintern journal in the spring of 1919, chairman Grigorii Zinoviev thought no-one would be surprised if by the time his article appeared there were not three, but 'six or more soviet republics'; and in a year's time they would 'already be beginning to forget that in Europe there was a struggle for socialism, for in a year all Europe will be communist'.

The Soviet republics in Bavaria and Hungary, however, soon collapsed, the risings in Germany and Bulgaria were ignominiously defeated, and the later 1920s saw authoritarian governments come to power throughout much of Europe; these governments then began to take action against their domestic communist and trade union movements. In China, what had been the most promising colonial revolutionary movement was crushed by Chiang Kai-shek in 1927, and elsewhere in the colonial world communist parties were enjoying little success. The USSR, as a result, was left almost entirely isolated as the world's first communist state for most of the period up to the Second World War, and its leadership became increasingly concerned to develop the country's military and industrial potential so that it could safely survive within this 'capitalist encirclement'. Trotsky, who still favoured a revolutionary foreign policy, was outmanoeuvred, expelled from the party and then (in 1929) forced into foreign exile; Stalin, who had become the party's General Secretary in 1922, went on to establish not just a personal ascendancy but a regime based on repression and terror, with millions in labour camps and leading oppositionists condemned to death in a series of show trials.

The only important respect in which Soviet isolation lessened during this period was with the establishment of people's republics in the small Siberian region of Tannu Tuva in 1921 (it was absorbed into the USSR as an autonomous province in 1944) and Mongolia in 1924, after Chinese occupying forces had been defeated with substantial Soviet assistance and the monarchy had been abolished. In all essentials, however, the USSR remained an isolated outpost of communism in international politics. The dangers of this isolation became steadily more apparent as the Western powers offered no serious resistance to the rise of Hitler, above all at Munich in 1938. A Nazi–Soviet non-aggression pact was signed in 1939, but in 1941 Hitler abruptly broke it off and invaded the western USSR. In the four years that followed the USSR lost over 27 million dead and suffered material damage on an unimaginable scale. There must have seemed every reason, as the end of the war approached, for Soviet negotiators to try to strengthen the security of their frontiers, above all in the west, and to make every effort to retain control over the parts of Eastern and Central Europe that they had liberated from the Nazis.

At the Moscow, Yalta and Potsdam conferences of 1944 and 1945 these objectives were substantially achieved, in large part with the acquiescence of the USSR's Western Allies, and the establishment of a system of communist states in Eastern Europe under Soviet control was essentially a product of the division of Europe into rival spheres of influence that was the outcome of these agreements. The Sovietisation of Eastern Europe took several forms, reflecting the strength of domestic support for a change of regime and the manner in which the countries concerned had been liberated from Nazi rule. All, however, were to become 'people's republics' in the short term, seen as a form of rule that was an intermediate stage towards a fully communist system. All (except Yugoslavia) became members of the economic and military alliances that the USSR had established within the region. And, with local variations, the political system in each of the East European states went through a similar process of Sovietisation. In the first stage, government was concentrated in the hands of the parties of the left and centre-left that had led the struggle against fascism; in the second stage these genuine coalitions were converted into bogus ones within which communists were dominant; and then came a third stage in which a communist political monopoly was established and any remaining elements of independence were extinguished within the party as well as outside it, leaving a uniformly communist local leadership that was entirely beholden to Moscow.

In several cases there had been little initial support for communist policies and the new government was effectively installed by the Red Army: for instance, in the German Democratic Republic, Poland and Romania. The GDR was something of a special case, in that it was part of a defeated Germany that had been allocated to the Soviet sphere of influence. Former Nazis were ousted from positions of power and an extensive programme of nationalisation and collectivisation was carried out; political parties, equally, were permitted to re-establish themselves, and then in 1946 the Communist and Social Democratic parties were merged into a Socialist Unity Party within which the former communist elements swiftly became dominant. In October 1949 a German Democratic Republic was established under party leadership, and by the end of the year it had been recognised by the USSR and the other communist powers.

Poland was the largest of the USSR's western neighbours with the longest common frontier, and as the war drew to a close it became increasingly clear that the Soviet authorities would insist on adding it to their sphere of influence in spite of the lack of domestic support for a communist administration. A series of boundary changes allocated a large part of the republic's eastern territory to the USSR, while Poland was awarded parts of eastern Germany in compensation; it was also agreed that a democratic government friendly to the USSR would be established. The Yalta agreement, on which these arrangements were based, had also provided for free elections, but the elections that were held in 1947 were heavily influenced by the authorities and they produced an overwhelming communist majority. A new president was elected – Bolesław Bierut, a Comintern official who was a citizen of the USSR; the new government began to nationalise large-scale industry, although little was done to collectivise agriculture; and a system of rule was established that was dominated by the Polish United Workers' Party, which had been formed (as in East Germany) by a compulsory merger of communists and socialists.

Romania had entered the Second World War in 1941 on the side of the Axis powers, but in 1944, after two Red Army groups had entered the country, its military government was overthrown and it changed sides in favour of the Allies. A communist-led government was established in 1945; a more decisive change followed in 1947 when the king was forced to abdicate, political opponents were arrested and Romania was declared a people's republic with a constitution (adopted in the spring of 1948) that was directly modelled on that of the USSR. Nationalisation of industry and natural resources took place under a law of 1948, and a formal system of state planning was initiated; agriculture, from 1949 onwards, was collectivised. Decisive in these developments was the Romanian Workers' Party, led from 1945 by Gheorghe Gheorghiu-Dej and merged with the socialists along familiar lines in 1948; Gheorghiu-Dej himself became prime minister as well as party leader in 1952 when the left-wing agrarian who had led the government up to this point was obliged to resign.

Bulgaria had also entered the war on the side of the Axis powers with the aim of satisfying its territorial ambitions. But in September 1944 Soviet troops entered the country and a coalition of anti-Nazi parties, formed the previous year, took this opportunity to seize power and declare war on Germany. Originally a minority within this new government, the Bulgarian Communist Party used its control of key ministries and Soviet support to become dominant within it and then to launch a determined campaign against real or alleged Nazi sympathisers in which tens of thousands were summarily executed. The monarchy was abolished after a plebiscite in 1946, and in 1947 a new constitution was adopted that declared Bulgaria a people's republic with Georgi Dimitrov – who had led the unsuccessful rising in 1923 and then became the hero of the Reichstag fire trial of 1933 – as its prime minister. In 1948 what remained of the Socialist Party merged with the communists, and in 1949 the first of Bulgaria's Five-Year Plans was put into effect. Although public opinion was strongly pro-Russian, the imposition of communist rule had taken place with particular brutality.

In Czechoslovakia and Hungary, as in Bulgaria, the communist party had traditionally enjoyed a substantial degree of popular support, and the Red Army, in spite of some excesses, was seen by many as the agency by which these countries had been liberated from the Nazis. Soviet forces entered Czechoslovakia in April 1944, together with a coalition government headed by the prewar president Edvard Beneš; the fall of Prague, in May 1945, marked the end of military operations in Europe. In the elections that took place in May 1946 the communists emerged as the largest party, with 38 per cent of the votes, and they were the most substantial element in a coalition government that was formed under the premiership of their leader Klement Gottwald. Beneš was elected president, but communists increased their influence and by 1948, after the resignation of a number of the ministers from other parties, they had become dominant. Later that year Czechoslovakia was declared a people's republic under a new constitution, the socialist and communist parties were merged, and Gottwald became president on Beneš's resignation. In January 1949 the country's first Five-Year Plan went into effect, dedicated to removing 'all traces of capitalism' from its economy.

Hungary had also entered the war on the side of the Axis powers, hoping (like Bulgaria) to reverse some of the boundary changes that had taken place after the First World War. But when the Hungarian government began to consider changing sides in 1944 the country was occupied by the Germans and a puppet government was installed in its place. Soviet troops entered the country later in the year, and it was liberated from Nazi rule in April 1945. The Hungarian Communist Party, banned before the war, had been re-established in Moscow under the leadership of Mátyás Rákosi, and he took this opportunity to return to Hungary and set up a broadly representative government. The Communist Party fared badly in the elections that took place in 1945, winning 17 per cent of the vote, and not much better under the less freely conducted elections of 1947, with 22 per cent, but they used their position to marginalise other parties and force them out of existence – it was Rákosi who invented these 'salami tactics' – and by 1948 they had established full control. In June 1948 another forced merger took place between the communists and the social democrats, and in 1949 a new constitution brought Hungary into the ranks of the people's democracies.

Things were rather different in Yugoslavia and Albania, where the Communist Party came to power through its leadership of a popular resistance movement against the Axis powers. In 1941 German forces had invaded Yugoslavia, where they swiftly set up a number of puppet regimes; but Yugoslav troops put up a continuing resistance from their mountain strongholds, with the most resolute opposition coming from Josip Tito's communist partisans. Tito enjoyed the support of the USSR, but also of the United Kingdom (Churchill wanted only to know 'who was killing the most Nazis'), and by late 1944 he and his guerrilla movement had forced the Germans into an embarrassing withdrawal. The Red Army entered Belgrade at this point, Tito's council of national liberation was merged with the royal government, and in March 1945 he became premier. But if the Red Army was the agency by which the communists acquired power, it is also clear that the latter enjoyed a measure of genuine support as the leaders of a successful liberation movement – support on which they were able to draw at a later stage when their policies diverged from Soviet orthodoxy. National elections in November 1945 gave an overwhelming majority to the communist-dominated People's Front, a constituent assembly abolished the monarchy, and Yugoslavia became a federal republic.

A new constitution, adopted in 1946 and modelled on the constitution of the USSR, gave broad powers to six constituent republics and two autonomous regions, reflecting the country's ethnic variety, but real power remained in the hands of Tito and the Communist Party. A vigorous programme of nationalisation was instituted, and a first Five-Year Plan, introduced in 1947, laid down an ambitious strategy for industrialisation; by the end of the decade a greater proportion of industry, agriculture and commerce had been taken into public ownership than in any other of the people's democracies. But relations with the USSR and the other communist powers, initially close, began to founder; and this left little alternative but to conduct a more independent foreign policy, and to depart from unpopular Stalinist policies at home. In 1950, symbolising this new departure, the first law on 'self-management' was adopted, vesting the direction of enterprises (at least nominally) in those who worked in them. More fundamentally, Yugoslavian theorists began to develop a critique of the USSR as a system, and of the way in which a privileged bureaucracy had become dominant within it.

In Albania, similarly, communists had come to power in November 1944 as the successful leaders of a wartime resistance movement, not 'in the baggage train of the Red Army'. Elections took place in December 1945 at which the communist-controlled Democratic Front won 93 per cent of the vote; in January 1946 the newly elected national assembly abolished the monarchy and declared Albania a people's republic; and in March 1946 a new constitution was adopted that was modelled on Yugoslavia's. The Yugoslavian embrace, originally, was all but overpowering; but party leader Enver Hoxha used the deterioration of Yugoslavia's relations with the other communist powers to establish closer relations of his own, and at the same time to eliminate the pro-Yugoslavian elements in the party leadership (who were executed in the summer of 1949). Albania, in effect, had become a client of the USSR and its allies rather than of its Balkan neighbour, and Hoxha had established an unchallenged domestic ascendancy.

THE PATTERN OF COMMUNIST RULE

Communist rule, by this time, had developed a number of characteristic features. In the first place, all of the communist states based themselves on an official ideology, Marxism–Leninism, which was derived from the theories of Marx, Engels and Lenin, and from Stalin up to the 1950s, and in China from Mao Zedong. It was the official ideology that provided the vocabulary of politics in these states, as well as the basis upon which their rulers claimed to exercise authority. Individual members of these societies, clearly, subscribed to a variety of views; Poland, for instance, was overwhelmingly Roman Catholic, with high levels of attendance at weekly mass. But its constitution committed all Polish citizens to a 'struggle still further to improve social conditions, to eliminate completely the exploitation of man by man, and to put into effect the great ideals of socialism'. There were similar commitments, in a variety of wordings, in the constitutions of the other communist-ruled countries; and in all of them there could be no direct challenge to official doctrines of this kind, although they could sometimes be interpreted with a degree of flexibility.

Second, in all these states factories, farms and other productive resources were owned by the state in the name of the people as a whole. Private ownership still existed: of personal effects, of savings, of housing, and – most notably in Poland and Yugoslavia – of agricultural land. Some states, in the early years of communist rule, even guaranteed a private capitalist sector within the broader framework of state ownership and planning. But it was a fundamental principle of communist rule that no-one could 'exploit' the labour of anyone else, so there were no landlords or stockbrokers, no private employers or wage labourers, no millionaires and no paupers. As the Czechoslovakian constitution explained in a representative formulation, a socialist economic system 'exclude[d] any form of exploitation of man by man'; economic crises and unemployment had been ended, and liberated human labour had become the 'basic factor in the entire society'. The Soviet constitution claimed similarly that the establishment of socialism had 'put an end once and for all to exploitation of man by man, antagonisms between classes, and strife between nationalities'.

Not only was there public ownership; there was public control through a system of central planning. In Mongolia, for instance, the constitution made clear that economic life was 'determined and directed by a single state economic plan'. In Czechoslovakia, similarly, the 'entire national economy' was based on central planning, and in the USSR the economy was a 'single complex' which was managed on the basis of state plans of economic and social development. There was scope for a wide range of economic activities outside the framework of the plan, including handicrafts and even small businesses; but activities of this kind had to be 'useful', they could not involve the 'exploitation of other people's labour', and the state ensured that such activities served the 'interests of society' and took place 'within the limits of the socialist economic system'. This meant that in the USSR and the countries that were modelled on it there could be no private factories or farms, and no foreign investment; and, apart from cooperatives, virtually all economic activity took place within a framework of state control and ownership.

As well as a distinctive system of economic and social management, there was a distinctive form of government. It had several key elements. One of them was a single ruling party, or at any rate a dominant one, as several of the communist-ruled countries in Eastern Europe allowed other parties to exist although not to compete for power. The communist party's dominant position was more than a matter of convention: it was normally a formal constitutional provision. In Czechoslovakia, for instance, Article 4 of the 1960 Constitution made it clear that the 'guiding force in society and in the state' was the 'vanguard of the working class, the Communist Party of Czechoslovakia, a voluntary militant alliance of the most active and politically conscious citizens from the ranks of the workers, farmers and intelligentsia'. In Romania the 'leading political force of the whole of society' was the Romanian Communist Party; and in Mongolia, to quote another formulation, the 'guiding and directing force of society and of the state [was] the Mongolian People's Revolutionary Party, which [was] guided in its activities by the all-conquering theory of Marxism–Leninism'.

The party itself was based upon the principle of democratic centralism, which was meant to ensure that office-holders were accountable and that there was the broadest possible discussion before decisions were taken, but which then required each level of the party organisation to accept and implement the decisions of the level above it. This was an organisational principle that gave the leadership extraordinary powers in relation to the party as a whole; it meant that there could be no 'factions' or organised groups within party ranks that were opposed to its centrally determined policies, and it contributed to the emergence of a dominant leadership – normally the party's general secretary – whose statements were regarded as particularly authoritative. As the Czechoslovakian party explained in its rules, the party was based on the 'ideological and organisational unity and cohesion of its ranks', and 'any manifestation of factionalism or group activity' was incompatible with membership. The Soviet Communist Party, in another representative formulation, made it clear that any expression of factionalism or group activity was 'incompatible with Marxist–Leninist party loyalty and with remaining in the party'.

The party, moreover, played a 'leading role' in the wider society, which meant that it sought to control all forms of organised life, from elections and the administration of justice to sport and the creative arts. Again, several mechanisms were involved. One was the party's 'cadres policy', by which it controlled all appointments to positions of influence. Another was its control over the flow of information, including a detailed censorship whose existence was itself subject to censorship. The operation of the censorship office in

Poland became the best-known in the communist countries in the 1970s when an official from Krakow defected to the West, taking his instructions with him. All kinds of subjects – such as the Katyn massacre of 1940, when thousands of Polish officers had been shot by Soviet forces (see Chapter 4) – could not be mentioned at all; and there were bans on a range of other topics, including the potential dangers of chemical fertilisers and Polish meat exports to the USSR. The party's leading role also meant that it sought to guide the activities of secondary associations of all kinds, including trade unions, women's movements, youth associations and sports clubs. There was, in effect, no 'private life' outside the circle of family and close friends.

Citizens in the communist countries were nominally endowed with a series of political rights, including the right to vote and to be elected to representative bodies, together with freedom of speech, movement and assembly. However, elections were so closely regulated that there was never – at least in the early communist years – a choice of candidate, and this in turn reflected the fact that the right of nomination was limited to the communist party and other organisations – such as the trade unions – that were under its direct control. The right to demonstrate, similarly, could not be used (in the words of the Romanian constitution) 'for aims hostile to the socialist system and to the interests of the working people'. Men and women had equal rights, and were expected to take a full part in public life; but again (as in the Czechoslovakian constitution) freedoms of speech and the press were guaranteed insofar as they were 'consistent with the interests of the working people', which meant in practice that they were heavily qualified. In Poland, similarly, the establishment of associations whose aims were 'directed against the political or social system' was prohibited.

Communist rule was maintained internationally by a network of institutions and alliances. Comecon, the first of these, was set up in 1949 by the Soviet Union and the East European states largely as a response to the establishment of the Organisation for Economic Cooperation and Development by the major Western countries, and to their participation in the Marshall Plan for postwar reconstruction. Comecon was largely a paper organisation up to the 1950s. Its members included the USSR, Bulgaria, Czechoslovakia, the GDR, Hungary, Poland, Romania and Mongolia; Albania, a founding member, took no part after 1961, and Cuba and Vietnam became members in the 1970s. Yugoslavia, although not a member, held observer status and took part in the work of Comecon on matters of mutual interest. Comecon was ruled by a statute that came into force in 1960 which placed its decisions in the hands of an annual meeting of prime ministers and chief planners; but its decisions were not binding, and Comecon itself was more of a vehicle for the coordination of national economic policies through a series of 'concerted plans of multilateral measures' than an agency for integration.

The military side of the alliance was the Warsaw Treaty Organisation, founded in 1955 by a treaty between the governments of Bulgaria, Czechoslovakia, Hungary, the GDR, Poland, Romania and the USSR; Albania, again one of the founding members, took no part in the work of the organisation after 1962 and formally announced its withdrawal in 1968. The central element in the treaty was a collective defence obligation that required all of its members to come to the assistance of any single member in the event of external attack. There was a joint command, established in 1956, and a political consultative committee, which was supposed to meet twice a year for wider purposes; but there was little activity within the WTO framework in the early years of its existence, and it was seen as a largely symbolic response to the incorporation of West Germany into NATO. By the late 1960s, however, there was an increasing emphasis upon joint operations, and a new set of institutions was established, including a committee of defence ministers. The USSR, none the less, remained the dominant member, with the WTO headquarters located in Moscow and the USSR itself contributing a disproportionate share of the alliance's defence expenditure.

Soviet efforts to retain control over the wider world of communist parties and movements were less successful, if only because most of the parties concerned were in countries beyond their reach. The Comintern began to meet less frequently, and in 1943 it was dissolved; a Communist Information Bureau functioned briefly from 1948 to 1956, bringing together some of the ruling and non-ruling parties (see Chapter 3). Otherwise, the main organisational form the movement assumed was a series of international conferences of communist and workers' parties, three of which were held in 1957, 1960 and 1969. One indication of the declining measure of Soviet control was the fact that at the last of these conferences several ruling parties (the Yugoslavian, Albanian, Chinese, Vietnamese and North Korean) did not attend; and of the 75 parties that were present, only 61 could be persuaded to sign the final communiqué without conditions (five refused to do so altogether). In practice, the most important force that held the bloc together was Soviet control over the internal politics and security of its closest allies – a control that began to diminish from the mid-1950s as the USSR itself moved from Stalinist totalitarianism to more broadly based patterns of authoritarian rule.

3 'National communism' in Eastern Europe

Communist rule, by the early 1950s, had been established throughout Eastern Europe and beyond; but it helps to understand its collapse a generation later if we remember that it was contested in many of these countries from the outset. There were no overt challenges to communist rule in the USSR itself, and indeed it became clear in Hungary in 1956 (as later in Czechoslovakia in 1968) that Soviet forces would intervene whenever the party leadership thought communism in other countries was in danger. At the same time, it was developments in the USSR that provided the context for a move towards more consultative forms of politics throughout the bloc; and the entire communist system was shaken by Khrushchev's 'secret speech' to the 20th Congress of the Soviet Communist Party in 1956, in which he accused the former leader of a 'whole series of major and extremely grave perversions of party principles, or party democracy, and of revolutionary legality'. The Soviet leadership became more collective; there was a greater emphasis on 'socialist legality'; and a 'thaw' in literature allowed the publication of a series of writings on the Stalin period, including Alexander Solzhenitsyn's prison-camp memoir *One Day in the Life of Ivan Denisovich* (1962).

The death of Stalin, in March 1953, had an immediate effect throughout the region. Just three months later a wave of protest swept through East Germany, following a decision to eliminate small traders and collectivise agriculture that had led to food shortages. The Soviet leadership, at this point, counselled moderation; but party leader Walter Ulbricht called for a higher workrate so that the crisis could be overcome by increased production. Workers on the Stalinallee in East Berlin, enraged by these demands, downed tools on 16 June, and a wave of demonstrations spread throughout the city, the protesters demanding the resignation of the government and free elections, as well as the withdrawal of the original decision. Several thousand demonstrators tried to occupy government buildings; the red flag was torn down from the Brandenburg Gate and burned; the Soviet commandant declared a state of siege; and Soviet divisions had to be called in to restore order. But the revolt spread to other East German cities, with public demonstrations and seizures of party buildings; public order was only restored by further Soviet military intervention, and thousands of arrests.

In Czechoslovakia the death of Stalin, followed by a currency reform that had wiped out the savings of ordinary people, led to a workers' protest in the town of Plzeň at the end of May. Demonstrators took possession of the town for two days, demanding not only better material conditions but political change, including the overthrow of the government. Public order ultimately had to be restored by armed security forces. In Poland, too, the early post-Stalin years were unstable. The industrial city of Poznań erupted in June 1956, when workers at a locomotives and heavy machinery factory staged a demonstration that turned into a riot and finally a pitched battle between the rioters and armed detachments of the police. Soviet leaders denounced the revolt as the work of imperialist agents, but the Poles drew the rather different conclusion that it was due to genuine grievances at a large number of enterprises in the city, and popular pressure led to the recall of Władysław Gomułka, the party leader who had been forced out on charges of 'nationalism' in 1948. Gomułka, released quietly in 1954 and then elected party leader by a nearly unanimous vote in October 1956, used the occasion to insist that models of socialism could vary: they could take the Soviet, or the Yugoslavian, or quite different forms, and only practical experience could indicate which was the most appropriate in any case.

The most serious challenge to communist rule in the early post-Stalin years was in Hungary, where public order was eventually restored by Soviet tanks; but the dispute with Yugoslavia that emerged during these years was arguably of greater significance, in that it established the right of a local communist leadership to repudiate the authority of the Kremlin. And, more than this, it led to the articulation of an alternative model of socialism that had considerable influence outside the bloc itself. By the end of the 1950s, with the Chinese beginning to develop a still more formidable challenge to Kremlin leadership, it had become clear that the imposed unity of the Stalin years would never be restored. Indeed, the divisions that had arisen were already extending across the world communist movement, and not simply across the regimes in which communists held state power. Viewed in retrospect, there were relatively few years in which there was a sense of common purpose across a movement that assumed working people shared a single destiny; and when a common purpose did exist, it was because it could be imposed by Soviet authority.

THE HUNGARIAN REVOLT *

The Hungarian revolt of October 1956 was a direct reaction to the events that had taken place in Poznan the previous June. Mátyás Rákosi, a loyal Stalinist in power since 1949, had initially been prepared to face down the pressure for change. He called a Central Committee meeting at the end of June 1956 which in turn condemned the 'open opposition' that had been organised by Imre Nagy, a former premier who had been critical of Soviet influence on Hungarian domestic affairs. Rákosi went on to incite workers against Hungary's intellectuals, describing them as 'agents of the bourgeoisie', and began to consider the possibility of arresting oppositional politicians and banning their newspapers. Moscow, however, had turned against Stalinism by this time; two members of the Soviet leadership, Anastas Mikoyan and Mikhail Suslov, arrived shortly afterwards in Budapest, and Rákosi was persuaded to tender his resignation as party leader.

Rákosi's replacement, in the event, was a scarcely less discredited Stalinist, Ernö Gerö, and the appointment served only to demoralise Rákosi's supporters while at the same time it further alienated the opposition. There were more appointments to the party leadership, but they balanced Rákosi's opponents (such as the future party leader János Kádár) against those who had shared his views. As a result, official policies became even more ambiguous: a more rapid rehabilitation of the victims of the past and a greater role for the Hungarian parliament, but at the same time a continuation of collectivisation and of the traditional emphasis upon heavy industry. Nagy, for his part, became increasingly the focus for liberal and patriotic opinion, but he refused to set up a rival centre of power and continued to support 'Leninist principles of democratic centralism'.

Public opinion became increasingly polarised. Writers began to reject the party's more moderate proposals, and to demand 'complete freedom for literature'. A group of reform-minded intellectuals, the Petöfi Circle, resumed its discussions, and similar groups sprang up in university towns all over the country. The concessions made by Gerö, meanwhile, were taken as signs of weakness and confusion. Characteristically, the party leadership first refused a state funeral for László Rajk, who had led the party during the war and then joined the post-war government, but who had become the most prominent purge victim in 1949; then, on 6 October, it agreed to do so. More than 300,000 people marched through the streets of Budapest: schoolchildren, office staff, writers and workers. Nagy walked at the head of the procession, and it was he who embraced Rajk's widow. Nagy, evidently, had been able to mobilise the masses and control them; the Hungarian leadership, for its part, found they were completely out of touch, still seeking instructions

* This section draws heavily on the account of Hungarian born French Journalist Francois Fejto (see further reading).

from Moscow rather than developing the kind of 'national communism' that was already emerging in Poland and Yugoslavia.

The Soviet leadership, for its part, was already looking beyond Gerö and towards the more flexible figure of János Kádár. As the news of what was happening in Poland began to spread, it even appeared possible that a similar pattern of events could be repeated in Hungary, with a 'Hungarian path to socialism' a real possibility if reformist party leaders took their opportunities. The Petöfi Circle, certainly, was seeking a range of moderate reforms at this time, including an emergency meeting of the Central Committee with Nagy's participation, the expulsion of Rákosi, and 'even closer links with the USSR on the basis of the Leninist principle of absolute equality'. Student demands, however, were more strident: the withdrawal of Soviet troops, general elections on a multi-party basis and far-reaching economic reform. They also called for a big demonstration of solidarity with Poland on 23 October, and it was this that precipitated the uprising.

The demonstration was at first banned by the Ministry of the Interior. The writers, the Petöfi Circle and the students sent several delegations to the Central Committee to get the decision reversed; eventually the ban was lifted, and the demonstration took place. But instead of petering out, it grew in size. The political vacuum created by the decline in the authority of the party leadership had certainly been filled, but by an oppositional force and an unstable one. The crowd became increasingly unruly; a statue of Stalin in the centre of Budapest was overthrown, the offices of the national radio station were occupied, and the national flag was hoisted with the emblem of the people's republic removed. Gerö's only response was a maladroit speech in which he emphasised Hungary's debt to the Soviet Union and condemned the demonstration as extremist. The speech merely underlined his isolation.

During the evening, shots were heard near the radio building. The security police were unable to disperse the crowd, the government was unsure of the army, and the Central Committee, hastily convened, panicked and took two conflicting decisions. On the one hand, Nagy was nominated to fill the prime ministerial position; on the other, an appeal was made to the Soviet garrison to restore order. This left Nagy in power, but unable to carry out the tasks to which he was committed. He did his best to reconcile the conflicting pressures that bore upon him: limiting repression, but at the same time to removing Gerö and his associates from the party, while also persuading the Soviet garrison to withdraw and asking all concerned to accept him as a mediator. But matters had by now developed to a point where he was facing a national rebellion against foreign domination and communist rule.

The same two emissaries from the Soviet party, Mikoyan and Suslov, arrived on the evening of 24 October. They appeared accommodating. They admitted that the appeal to Soviet troops had been a mistake; Gerö was dismissed, and Kádár replaced him as party leader. Spokesmen for the writers urged the rebels to lay down their arms and give their support to Nagy and Kádár, who were starting to negotiate with a view to the formation of a more representative administration. But the street-fighting continued, the party began to fragment and the central government found it impossible to impose its authority. The strike was also extending to the provinces, in nearly all of which power passed into the hands of revolutionary committees and workers' councils.

A new government was announced by Nagy on 27 October, but it included too many figures from the old regime and as a result it failed to inspire confidence. Popular demands became increasingly radical, pressing openly for independence, free elections and the withdrawal of Soviet troops. Nagy himself was torn between the agreement with his Soviet interlocutors, which he basically regarded as satisfactory, and the popular groups with which he was also in contact. He tried to regain control by legalising the rebellion, ordering the police and the Russians to cease fire, but in turn he lost support within the party and state apparatus on which he depended for his position. He turned to the peasant and social democratic parties, which had some political experience, to help him recover control; and on 30 October he announced a return to a 'system of government based on the democratic cooperation of the coalition parties as they existed in 1945'. Nagy, apparently, believed this was compatible with a broad commitment to socialism; but the leaders of the uprising went even further, demanding withdrawal from the Warsaw Pact and complete neutrality. Eventually, he conceded.

Mikoyan and Suslov returned at this point to Budapest, apparently still committed to their earlier agreement. The calls for multi-party politics and a withdrawal from the Warsaw Pact, however, showed how much political ground had been covered in just a few days, and were enough to persuade a majority in the Kremlin that military intervention would have to be attempted. A national communist leader, like Gomułka, was one thing; but a neutral and Western-leaning Hungary was quite another. And it was clear that Western governments, in the end, would accept an intervention; Hungary, under the terms of the Yalta settlement, was in the Soviet sphere of influence, and in any case the West had its own business to attend to in Suez.

On 4 November Soviet troops regrouped around Budapest and began to advance. Red Army tanks opened fire on the barricades erected by the rebels. A few hours earlier, the authorised representatives of the Nagy government had been arrested. The Soviet intervention soon overcame the rebels' barricades, and the Hungarian army made no effort to support them. Workers from a few large factories, and miners, put up the strongest resistance. Hopes of Western assistance, however, were quickly disappointed. Soviet spokesmen justified their intervention by reference to the Warsaw Treaty, which allowed the USSR to protect Hungary against 'subversion'. Kádár, moreover, had appealed directly for the USSR's support, disowning Nagy in a radio broadcast on 4 November and announcing the formation of a new worker-peasant government. Kádár did not repudiate a popular movement that had begun to put right the 'anti-party and anti-democratic crimes committed by Rákosi and his associates', but the movement had been exploited by 'reactionary elements', workers and young people had been misled, and the whole country had been engulfed by 'excesses, murdering and looting'. In these difficult circumstances, Kádár and his colleagues had called for the assistance of the Red Army to 'smash the sinister forces of reaction and restore order and calm'.

It is difficult to be surprised, in retrospect, that an overt challenge to the socialist system in Hungary and to its international alliances led to external intervention. The Poles, under Gomułka, had moved towards 'national communism', within the framework of a socialist system and the country's international alliances, and with overwhelming popular support. The Hungarians, by contrast, were divided. Nagy was indecisive, and found himself pushed beyond the limits of what was politically feasible. Kádár was unwilling to contemplate more than the de-Stalinisation from above that was taking place at the same time in the USSR, while radicals had formed entirely new institutions, and were prepared to demand the replacement of communist rule by a multi-party democracy within a state that was neutral in its international allegiances. The outcome, in the short term, was external intervention and repression (Nagy himself was executed in 1958); although in the longer term Kádár moved to adopt most elements of Nagy's programme, except multi-party politics and neutrality, and pushed towards a reconciliation with a traumatised society.

YUGOSLAVIA, CHINA AND THE INTERNATIONAL DIMENSION

Communism was always an international movement. Workers, after all, 'had no country'. The Soviet government had itself begun as a revolutionary administration of workers and peasants, heading an association of revolutionary governments that sought in the last resort to abolish the state itself. There could be no suggestion, after the turmoil of the early post-revolutionary years, that capitalism was heading for an early demise; indeed, there might have to be an extended period of 'peaceful coexistence' (a term associated with Khrushchev, who wished to avoid a forcible resolution of the differences that must inevitably exist between two incompatible social orders). But in the long term there could be no doubt that socialism would prevail; and Soviet spokesmen lost no opportunity to point out that the 'correlation of forces' was moving steadily in their direction. Communist rule, after all, had been extended to Eastern Europe and much of Asia. The Western powers were meanwhile losing their position throughout the formerly colonial world, and increasing numbers were joining or voting for communist and workers' parties in the Western countries themselves (in many cases, it later emerged, Moscow had been helping them with covert financial support).

The first organisation that sought to bring together the parties of the left under Soviet auspices, the Communist International, had been dissolved during the war. In 1947 a new organisation was set up, the Communist Information Bureau or Cominform. It was in part a response to the more prominent place that the United States had assumed in Europe, and to the Marshall Plan in particular. Its purpose was to bring the European communist movement, including the parties of the people's democracies, under Soviet control, and its founding members were the communist parties of France and Italy, as well as the ruling parties of Bulgaria, Czechoslovakia, Hungary, Poland, Romania, the Soviet Union and Yugoslavia. The dissolution of the Comintern, Andrei Zhdanov told the Cominform's inaugural meeting, did not mean there should be no more organised contact among the fraternal parties: such mutual isolation would be 'wrong, harmful, and, in point of fact, unnatural'. One of the Cominform's early actions was to organise a campaign against the Yugoslavs, whose party leadership had 'taken the road of nationalism'. Stalin evidently thought the Yugoslavian leadership would be unable to survive in these circumstances: 'I have only to shake my little finger', he told Khrushchev, 'and there will be no more Tito'. But the Yugoslavs surmounted the crisis, and indeed began to develop a critique of a 'socialism of the apparatus' that provided a coherent alternative to those in the East European parties who were seeking to distance themselves from the political practice of Stalinism.

As Khrushchev told the 20th Party Congress, they had 'paid dearly for this "shaking of the little finger"', and it was one of the early objectives of his leadership to secure a reconciliation. Leading a delegation that included Prime Minister Bulganin, he flew to Belgrade in May 1955 and in a speech at the airport blamed the split on Stalin's immediate associates, who had based their decisions on materials that had been 'fabricated by enemies of the people'. The Soviet leadership, he indicated, wished to base its future relations on the principles of 'peaceful coexistence of states, on the principles of equality, non-interference, respect for sovereignty and national independence'. Tito, for his part, acknowledged his 'solidarity' with the other communist-ruled countries, but the declaration that was issued in June 1955 accepted the principles of 'mutual respect and non-intervention in internal affairs', and that the 'particular forms of developing socialism [were] exclusively a matter for the people of the countries in question'.

The 20th Congress of the Soviet Communist Party in early 1956 endorsed the rapprochement with Yugoslavia, calling for 'friendship and cooperation' with its 'friendly peoples', and it recognised that the forms of transition to socialism would be 'even more diverse' in the future – in particular between the USSR itself and the people's democracies. The Congress was warmly welcomed in Belgrade, and so too was the decision in April 1956 to dissolve the Cominform, whose decisions had given rise to the original dispute. When Tito came to Moscow in June 1956 it was as an ideological ally; he and Khrushchev signed a declaration that committed both sides to cooperation that was based on 'complete voluntariness and equality, friendly criticism and comradely exchange of opinions on matters in dispute', and which recognised that patterns of socialist development could vary from country to country and indeed that socialism was strengthened when they did so.

The other East European countries, given this Soviet lead, began to restore relations with Belgrade. Yugoslavian spokesmen, for their part, began to criticise 'little Stalins' in the other East European countries, and to support de-Stalinisation. There were several aspects of the Yugoslavian experience that national communists in other countries found of interest. One was the decollectivisation of agriculture; another was decentralisation; another was the struggle against bureaucracy; and a fourth were the workers' councils through which the Yugoslavian state was being administered. This was somewhat alarming to the Kremlin, which continued to insist in a confidential communication to other ruling parties that there could be close collaboration 'only with parties that [adhered] strictly to the doctrine of Marxism–Leninism'. But there could be no restoration of the unity that had once prevailed, and which had been based on Soviet domination; the Soviet government had itself to acknowledge, in October 1956, that 'errors' had been made in relations among the socialist countries, and that they had 'devalued the principles of legal equality between the socialist states in their relations with each other'.

Relations were meanwhile deteriorating with the other communist giant, the People's Republic of China. In the case of China, and to some extent elsewhere, there was in fact some doubt about whether local communists had enjoyed the backing of the Soviet government in attempting to proceed directly to the establishment of communist rule. Soviet representatives urged a truce with the Chinese Nationalists (the Kuomintang) until the last possible moment, and the Soviet ambassador was the last to leave the Nationalist government immediately before its downfall. The USSR none the less recognised the Chinese People's Republic on 2 October 1949, the day after its foundation, and in February 1950 the two countries concluded a friendship treaty with a thirty-year period of validity.

The Chinese leaders, however, appeared to have been dissatisfied with a number of aspects of the Sino-Soviet treaty, and at the 20th Congress of the CPSU they were reportedly unhappy about the manner in which the Stalin question had been handled. The Chinese, as late as 1957, still accepted Soviet leadership of the world communist movement (China, Mao conceded, had 'not even a quarter of a sputnik, whereas the Soviet Union [had] two'). Meanwhile, Soviet support for the Chinese atomic programme was withdrawn in 1958, the USSR was neutral during the Sino-Indian border conflict of 1959, and in 1960 the dispute between the USSR and China came into the open. Khrushchev, speaking at the Romanian Communist Party Congress in June of that year, attacked the Chinese leadership directly. All Soviet technicians were withdrawn; trade between the two countries dropped off sharply; and a series of hostile open letters was exchanged, the Chinese accusing the Russians of 'revisionism' (or lack of commitment to Marxist principles), while the Russians accused the Chinese of 'dogmatism' and 'splittism' (or of attempting to break up the world communist movement). In 1966 both sides recalled their ambassadors and in 1969 matters reached the point of military hostilities along the Sino-Soviet border in Siberia. Relations subsequently improved, but it still appeared unlikely, given their historic rivalries and often divergent interests, that the unity of earlier years would ever be restored.

There was better news from Latin America, where Fidel Castro had assumed power in 1959 with the overthrow of the Batista dictatorship. Castro's programme was initially of a broadly democratic character, and it did not have the direct support of the local communist party; but in December 1961 he publicly declared his allegiance to Marxism–Leninism, and the country moved subsequently into an increasingly close association with the other communist countries. Diplomatic relations with the USSR and its allies were established in 1960 and were broken off with the United States the following year, after American banks and landholdings had been seized. Khrushchev, speaking to the 22nd Congress of the CPSU in October 1961, was able to congratulate the Cubans on their defeat of an attempted invasion some months earlier when American mercenaries had been hurled into the Bay of Pigs – 'the right place for them', he added amid applause and laughter. Castro's was a guerrilla movement in power, not a conventional communist regime, but it gave the USSR a toehold in Latin America, within ninety miles of the US coastline, and provided a powerful impetus for radical politics throughout the region.

4   The limits of reform

In the 1960s it was still possible to conceive of a communist rule that was not simply 'national' but based upon an accommodation with the society over which it ruled. The intervention of Soviet troops in Hungary had made it clear that no direct challenge would be permitted to the security of the bloc as a whole, in that country or elsewhere. But it did not preclude an attempt to broaden the basis on which communist governments interacted with their societies: Kádár, indeed, was of the first to begin a dialogue with his traumatised country on the basis of his celebrated principle that 'whoever is not against us is with us'. There was no suggestion that the party's leading role should be abandoned or qualified in any way, but its leadership became more tolerant and a dialogue developed between the party and other organised interests that allowed at least a cautious questioning of official policies. Hungary was also one of the first of the communist countries to establish an element of electoral choice, with the introduction of independent candidatures in 1967; it was a practice that became universal in the early 1980s.

In the USSR, by contrast, the liberalisation that had taken place under Khrushchev began to give way to a greater degree of orthodoxy. A decision was taken in 1964 to avoid the danger of an undue concentration of power in the hands of a single person by separating the party leadership and the prime ministership (Khrushchev had combined them between 1958 and 1964). The leadership itself became more collective, although Leonid Brezhnev was certainly its most prominent individual member; it was a leadership that brought together representatives of the country's most important institutions and regions as well as the most senior party officials, and it operated in an increasingly institutionalised way. But dissidents were harshly treated (two of the most prominent, the writers Yuli Daniel and Andrei Sinyavsky, were put on trial in 1966 on charges of slandering the Soviet system); economic reform ground to a halt after the 'Kosygin reforms' of the mid-1960s had encouraged enterprises to earn profits on their activities; and in 1977 a new constitution gave added force to party dominance by providing for its leading role in an entirely new article.

There were unlikely to be changes, in such circumstances, in the relations among communist states during the period that followed the suppression of the Hungarian uprising. On the contrary, attempts were made to forge a greater degree of unity across the bloc through (for instance) a programme for the further development of 'socialist economic integration' that was approved by Comecon in 1971, and a series of reforms within the Warsaw Treaty Organisation that gave it a committee of defence ministers, a committee of foreign ministers and a reorganised joint secretariat in the late 1960s and 1970s. But there was a greater diversity in domestic affairs as East European governments embarked on market-oriented economic reform, and many of them began to explore what scope there might be for a form of rule that would have allowed a greater degree of consultation with their societies if not a general election that would allow them to be dismissed from office. The crushing of the Prague Spring in 1968 and the suppression of Solidarity in Poland at the start of the 1980s made it clear that domestic changes of this kind could go too far for the Soviet leadership even if there was no formal challenge to the leading role of the party or to the system of alliances on which the bloc was based. Ironically, it was Soviet intervention 'in defence of socialism' that made it impossible to explore what scope there might have been for a form of communist rule that rested upon popular consent, which in the long run was the only basis on which it could have hoped to survive.

THE PRAGUE SPRING OF 1968

The most far-reaching attempt within this period to establish a different model of communist rule was Czechoslavakia's 'Prague Spring' (although the popular title of the reform movement is something of a misnomer as it embraced the whole country and lasted most of the year). The origins of the reform movement lay deep in Czechoslovakian history. The country had been the only East European state that had maintained democracy throughout the interwar period; in Poland, for instance, Piłsudski had staged a coup in 1926 that established a military dictatorship, and some of the others were overtly fascist. But in Czechoslovakia there were genuine elections, the press continued to express a variety of viewpoints, the courts were independent and the country's religious denominations were left undisturbed. Not less important for later developments, the Czechoslovakian Communist Party reflected the same traditions: it was parliamentary in its orientation, had a substantial membership and could normally command a substantial vote at the elections in which its candidates took part.

There was clearly a sharp divergence between these liberal, pluralistic traditions and the centralised form of Stalinist rule that was imposed after

1948. For Klement Gottwald, party leader from 1929 up to his death in 1953, the Soviet Union was 'our model'. There was no real de-Stalinisation; nor was this surprising, as party leader Antonín Novotný, who came to power later in 1953, had made an active contribution to the purges – the most extensive in Eastern Europe – in his ascent to power. Characteristically, a statue of Stalin on the outskirts of Prague was the largest outside the USSR, and the last (in 1962) to be dismantled. The new constitution that was adopted in 1960, similarly, was strongly centralist: it declared the party the 'leading force in society and in the state' and claimed that Czechoslovakia was already socialist and that it would soon make a transition to communism (it was the first of the East European countries to make this claim).

Czechoslovakia was one of the multinational communist states, and the pressure for a looser relationship between the Czech lands and other parts of the country was one of the most important forces that contributed to the Prague Spring. Czechoslovakia was predominantly Czech (about 66 per cent), but the Slovaks (29 per cent) were a substantial minority. The Czech lands, before the First World War, had been part of Austria; Slovakia part of Hungary. The Czech lands, equally, were more industrialised, with higher living standards; Slovakia was agrarian, poorer and more traditionally Catholic. In the 1950s there had been a campaign against Slovak nationalism; but by the 1960s the communist party in Slovakia, and still more openly the writers' union, was pressing for a genuine federation with extensive powers of local self-government, and attacking a 'Czechoslovakism' that meant unmediated rule from Prague.

It was the economy, however, that most directly precipitated change. A leading industrial power before the war, Czechoslovakia began to experience an economic slowdown in the 1960s. In 1962 and 1963 there were falls, rather than increases, in national income; serious shortages began to emerge, the Five-Year Plan had to be abandoned, and in 1962 a new One-Year Plan was introduced in its place. At the end of 1963 a commission was established by the party authorities to consider a range of possible ways forward; it included Ota Šik, head of the Institute of Economics of the Academy of Sciences and a member of the party's Central Committee. Its proposals, approved in various stages from 1964 onwards, involved a partial move towards the market, with a greater role for profits as an indicator of success, a convertible currency and much larger wage differentials.

The Prague Spring owed much of its inspiration, in addition, to the intellectual ferment that swept through virtually every field of cultural endeavour. The Union of Czechoslovak Writers and its paper *Literární noviny* (*Literary News*) were central foci. There was a stormy Congress in 1963, with open attacks on Stalinism. And in 1967, at the writers' 4th Congress, there were direct attacks on the party leadership, and on censorship in all its forms; the

Congress, in its closing resolution, spoke of the need for a far-reaching 'democratisation of human values'. There was a parallel revival of interest in Franz Kafka, a Czech-Jewish writer whose accounts of impersonal bureaucracies began to appear strikingly relevant to the institutional forms of communist rule. Historians began to reject the imposition of a party line; sociologists began to use opinion polls to discover what people really thought, and to explore the inequalities that still persisted in what was nominally a socialist society. The official youth movement began to lose members, and there was an angry candlelit demonstration in October 1967 when the heat and light failed in a college dormitory.

The reform movement that emerged into the open during 1968 accelerated during the year, once Novotný had ceded the leadership to the Slovak First Secretary Alexander Dubček in January. There were no direct attacks on socialism, the leading role of the Communist Party, or on membership of the Warsaw Treaty Organisation. But a process of reform began to gather pace, much of it expressed in an Action Programme that was adopted by the Communist Party's Central Committee in April 1968. The Action Programme was an eclectic document that took its inspiration from several different sources; and it was often declaratory, in that it promised subsequent reform but did not make a more specific commitment. There would, for instance, be a new constitution, but later. There would be a new electoral law, but it had not been drafted by the time the Warsaw Pact forces invaded in August. The new programme was most convincing as a general statement of the reformers' objective: a 'new profoundly democratic model of Czechoslovakian socialism conforming to Czechoslovakian conditions'.

It followed immediately that the Communist Party should no longer – as the Action Programme put it – 'rule over society', but rather that it should earn the right to play a leading role by the strength of its policies and the personal example of its members. This meant a rather different party, one that had fully democratised its own activities. A new set of party rules, later in the year, began to make a reality of some of these general objectives. The party became a federal one, with a Central Committee that was to be a 'party parliament', and with greater powers for the Slovaks. Lateral or 'horizontal' links between party branches were approved, instead of being defined as a deviation from democratic centralism. Minority rights, at the same time, were enhanced: minorities had to accept majority decisions, but they had the right to retain their original opinions and to reopen the issue if circumstances changed. And there would be secret and competitive elections for leading party positions, which themselves would be held for a limited period (the new party rules were adopted in August 1968, just before the whole reform movement was crushed by external intervention, and so they were never put into effect).

The Communist Party had traditionally headed a single electoral list with the country's other legal but not competitive political parties. This, the 'National Front', was to become a genuine partnership, with equal rights for each of its members. The national assembly that they elected was to become a 'genuine socialist parliament'. There was to be a separation of powers, a more independent legal system, and a security service that was no longer to intervene in domestic political questions. The victims of earlier years were to be rehabilitated; a law was adopted in June that provided for the review of all the sentences that had been passed on political oppositionists from 1948 to 1965. A new federal system was introduced during the year, with much greater powers for the Slovaks and a federal as well as republican parliaments.

Freedoms of speech, association and assembly were to be defined in subsequent legislation which would also define what was meant by 'anti-social' associations. Ordinary people, meanwhile, began to set up the kinds of organisation they wanted. There was K231, named after the article of the criminal code under which political oppositionists had been sentenced in the past; and KAN, a 'club of non-party activists' that was close to an independent political party. A new press law was promised in the Action Programme; the existing law was extensively modified in June, and censorship in its original form was ended – an event without precedent in the communist world, and one that was viewed with understandable concern by the leaderships of neighbouring states. Freedom of movement was also conceded, including the right to take up residence abroad.

The Action Programme referred in more general terms to the economy, where it would seek to establish a 'socialist market suitably combined with central planning'. There were references to the 'humanistic mission of culture', and a more cautious reference to foreign policy, where Czechoslovakia would take its 'own stand' but on the basis of an association with the other communist-ruled states that was 'fundamental'. There was no suggestion in the Action Programme of independent parties or trade unions; there was no serious criticism of collective agriculture, which undeniably worked reasonably well; and there was no indication that the party would relinquish its ultimate control over appointments. This was none the less a distinct conception of reform – 'socialism with a human face', as it came to be known – and the opinion polls that were conducted at the time suggested it was a programme that satisfied the aspirations of a very large majority of Czechs and Slovaks.

The direction of change in Czechoslovakia was less welcome in the other communist states, even though there had been no direct challenge to the country's international alliances or to the leading role within it of the Communist Party. What, for instance, if the party lost effective control, even if it did not directly abandon its position of ultimate authority? And what if it lost its control over the media, for so long a mainstay of communist rule? This was not an abstract danger, as the publication in June of a liberal manifesto, 'Two Thousand Words', made clear. The party, it suggested, had lost the trust it had once commanded. Those who had abused office should now be forced to retire and the public should combine in various ways to ensure that the reforms continued, whatever the 'party–state bureaucracy' might wish. It was a statement, charged the Soviet party newspaper *Pravda*, that sought to 'discredit the Czechoslovakian Communist Party and its leading role, to undermine the friendship between the Czechoslovakian people and the peoples of fraternal socialist states, and to pave the way for counter-revolution'.

The same concerns were evident in an open letter to the Czechoslovakian party that was approved by the Soviet and four other ruling parties in mid-July, and which rehearsed the justification that would later be presented for military intervention. Developments in Czechoslovakia, they began, had aroused 'profound anxiety'. The 'forces of counter-revolution, supported by imperialist centres', had 'launched a broad offensive against the socialist system without encountering the requisite opposition'. The party itself was 'losing control over the course of events'; the frontiers of socialism were accordingly at risk; and 'healthy forces' must now be rallied, which could count on the 'solidarity and comprehensive assistance of the fraternal socialist countries'. The Czechs, in reply, insisted they would not allow the 'historic achievements of socialism' to be threatened, but for the Soviet Communist Party this simply confirmed the depth of their failure to understand the threat they now confronted. Could one wait, they asked, until counter-revolutionary forces had gained control of the situation in Czechoslovakia before giving battle to them?

Intervention followed on 21 August, the USSR leading East German, Polish, Bulgarian and Hungarian forces to suppress what they described as a 'silent counter-revolution'. As an editorial in *Pravda* made clear, the 'defence of socialism [was] the highest international duty': if the 'achievements of socialism' were threatened in any individual country, the other socialist countries would be entitled and indeed obliged to intervene. This was what became known as 'socialist internationalism', a term that entered the Soviet constitution in 1977. It was known in the West as the 'Brezhnev Doctrine'. As the Soviet leader put it, speaking to the Polish Party Congress in November 1968, any threat to communist rule would be considered 'not only a problem of the people of the country in question, but a general problem and concern of all the socialist countries'. The result was that Czechoslovakia became the 'world's most peace-loving country': not only did it not intervene in the internal affairs of other countries, it didn't even intervene in its *own* internal affairs.

POLAND AND SOLIDARITY

Stalin is reported to have remarked that to introduce communism in Poland was like putting a saddle on a cow. There were certainly all kinds of cultural factors that suggested that political authoritarianism, especially if it emanated from Russia, would be an unsuccessful transplant. Poland, for a start, was a part of the Western cultural tradition. Its legal system drew on the heritage of Roman law, with its concepts of private property and of a set of civil rights that could not be infringed by government or other citizens. It had been a part of the great movements of European history, including the Renaissance and the Reformation. A Pole, Nicolas Copernicus, had made a particularly outstanding contribution to the development of modern astronomy. A Polish king, Jan Sobieski, had saved Christian Europe from the advancing Turks in front of Vienna in the late seventeenth century. Poles, moreover, were very conscious of the ways in which they shared a common European heritage, and they were inclined (perhaps too readily) to believe they were the eastern frontier of Europe, or even of civilisation, with the countries beyond them essentially Asian.

Poland's particular relationship with the outside world had much to do with its Roman Catholicism. The Church was closely identified with the nation; indeed, during the periods in which an independent Poland had entirely disappeared from the map, it was the Church that had preserved a sense of nationhood. The same kind of identification of Church and nation was encouraged by the periodic attempts that were made to suppress Polish nationhood and to persuade them to leave their historic faith by their neighbours, Lutheran Germany and Orthodox Russia. The changes that had taken place in Polish boundaries had left them, after 1945, overwhelmingly Polish by nationality and Catholic by religious faith – about 95 per cent of the population was classified as Catholic, and levels of observance were extremely high in comparative terms (over half of the population in the 1980s were regular communicants; about 80 per cent of Communist Party members were reportedly believers).

The Church, moreover, had a central place in public life. There was a full hierarchy, with five cardinals, eighty bishops and more than 20,000 priests, which was more than twice as many as in 1945. There was a Catholic university, at Lublin; there were Catholic chaplains in the armed forces; there were Catholic newspapers; and there were Catholic political parties, although they were not directly competitive with the communists. The place of Catholicism in national life was enormously enhanced by the election in 1978 of the Archbishop of Krakow, Karol Wojtyła, as Pope John Paul II. When the newly elected Pope visited his native country in the summer of 1979 about a quarter of the population was reported to have attended; the crowds at the meeting in Krakow on his departure numbered nearly 2 million.

Poles who identified themselves as Catholics were, of course, expressing more than their religious convictions; it was also a way of reflecting their nationhood. This meant, in practice, their hostility to Russians, and for all kinds of understandable historical reasons. Russia had taken part, in the eighteenth century, in the three partitions that had eventually eliminated Poland from the map. Poland had been absorbed within the Russian Empire after 1815, first as a personal union of crowns, and then as an ordinary province after uprisings in 1830 and 1863–4, when the kingdom and name of Poland were abolished and the area was subject to intense Russification. Poland regained its independence in 1918, but a Russo-Polish war broke out almost immediately when Polish troops invaded Russia; they were thrown back from the gates of Kiev, and then the Red Army reached as far as Warsaw before a peace treaty was concluded in 1921 that essentially restored the previous boundary.

Poland suffered once again as a 'land in between' when the Nazi–Soviet Pact was concluded in 1939; in a secret protocol it was divided between its two more powerful neighbours, and more than a million Poles were deported when Soviet forces occupied the eastern part of the country. Poland suffered still heavier losses during the war itself, when it was occupied from the outset by the Nazis and then painfully liberated: of the 18 million Nazi victims in all countries, an estimated 11 million died on occupied Polish territory (of these, over 5 million were Jews). Among many war crimes, one had enormous significance for Polish–Soviet relations: the discovery in April 1943 of the bodies of over 4,000 Polish officers at Katyn, near Smolensk. They had been among the 15,000 Polish officers deported from Poland by Soviet forces in 1939, and from whom nothing had been heard since 1940. The Nazis blamed the Red Army; the Soviet authorities blamed the Nazis, but refused to allow an investigation by the International Red Cross. Years later this was one of the issues that Gorbachev sought to defuse by establishing a joint commission of historians to discover the truth; Poles did not have to wait so long to draw their own conclusions.

Long-term factors of this kind were certainly important, but they were not in themselves decisive. A further contribution was made by the ineptitude with which the Polish authorities made their decisions. Most notably, in December 1970, less than two weeks before Christmas, there were sharp rises in the prices of meat and other foodstuffs. Riots broke out, particularly in the northern port cities, and Communist Party offices were attacked. After the army had been brought in and innocent workers had been shot dead, there were wholesale changes in the party and state leadership (this was the first time in any country that public pressure had led directly to the replacement of a communist administration). The new party leader, Edward Gierek, was a Silesian miner who appeared to have a better understanding of the problems of ordinary people; he appealed directly to the shipyard workers for the opportunity to make a fresh start and appeared for some time to have gained their confidence.

The old food prices were restored in February 1971; and for a couple of years there were high rates of growth as Poland invested heavily in new productive capacity aimed at export markets. But there was heavy foreign borrowing to finance this investment, which had to be paid for out of export earnings. These became more difficult to sustain after the sudden rise in the world price of oil in the early 1970s had cut the purchasing power of Western markets, while at the same time leading to raised interest rates and increasing the cost of servicing foreign borrowings. Equally, higher money earnings at home combined with fixed prices led to an increasingly heavy burden of subsidy and growing shortages. An attempt was made to resolve these tensions in 1976 when further price rises were proposed, but there were spontaneous public demonstrations and the measures were withdrawn for further consideration. The economy continued to deteriorate: national income fell by 2 per cent in 1979, and export earnings dropped below the level that was necessary just to service the foreign debt, let alone begin to repay it. Meanwhile, an increasingly well-organised opposition was developing in the shipyards, around independent publishing houses and within the political space that was provided by the Church.

The immediate source of the crisis that gave rise to Solidarity was once again an increase in the price of meat, in the summer of 1980. Work stopped all over the country; there was an occupation strike in the Lenin Shipyard in Gdansk; and a stocky, moustachioed electrician called Lech Wałęsa emerged to lead the opposition, becoming chairman of an inter-enterprise strike committee. The authorities had no alternative but to negotiate, and an agreement was eventually hammered out at the end of August that reflected the varied nature of the strikers' demands and of popular concerns more generally. It was agreed to establish 'new self-governing trade unions that would genuinely represent the working class'; the mass media would reflect a variety of viewpoints and broadcast the Sunday mass; there would be a general wage increase, a shorter working week and major improvements in the public services. Solidarity was formally an independent trade union, but one that was closer to a national resistance movement; it accepted a formulation in November that placed it under the nominal authority of the Communist Party, but it was far from clear what relationship could be established between a genuinely independent popular movement and a communist party that still insisted on its dominant position.

Both sides, in the event, moved further apart over the months that followed.

There were far-reaching changes in the party leadership: Gierek suffered a heart attack and a new leader took his place, Stanisław Kania, who was committed to a loosely defined 'renewal' that was intended to restore the party's credibility through a measure of internal democratisation. The party, in the event, began to fragment and lose any sense of purpose. Membership began to fall; and those who remained moved in different directions, some joining Solidarity itself and others favouring the restoration of communist orthodoxy. All of these developments, at the same time, had international implications. The Soviet authorities made their concerns abundantly clear in an open letter that was addressed to the Polish Party's Central Committee in June 1981: it warned of 'counter-revolution' and called on Polish comrades to 'reverse the course of developments'. If they failed to do so it was clear there would be a real danger of external intervention, with incalculable consequences in a large European country with a well-organised army.

Solidarity itself was changing at the same time. It acquired a national membership of about 10 million, out of a total workforce of 13 million; a counterpart, Rural Solidarity, was formed in the countryside; and its leadership became increasingly militant as the country's economic difficulties – which they saw as essentially political – became more serious (national income fell by 6 per cent in 1980 and rationing, even of vodka, became widespread). By September and October 1981 there were calls within Solidarity for the formation of a workers' militia, and for free multi-party elections to a new parliament; Lech Wałęsa had to face a serious challenge for the leadership, and won no more than 55 per cent against more uncompromising opponents. Solidarity's programme, adopted at this time, was a strikingly eclectic document: there were welfarist elements in its calls for social justice, but it was strongly Catholic and liberal in its commitment to multi-party politics and the rule of law. It was not easy, by this stage, to see what basis there could be for a lasting accommodation between Solidarity's increasingly radical demands and the party authorities, who were themselves under pressure from their Warsaw Pact allies.

These tensions were resolved, in the event, by the declaration of a state of martial law on 13 December 1981, supposedly to restore public order. Wojciech Jaruzelski, the general who had become Prime Minister in February 1981 and then party leader in October, was later to represent his actions as those of a responsible patriot anxious to avoid the loss of life that would have attended a Warsaw Pact invasion. But lives were lost as workers refused to be cowed; 10,000 were interned during the first year of martial rule, including Lech Wałęsa and the other Solidarity leaders; Solidarity itself was suspended, and then suppressed; the party was purged of Solidarity sympathisers or members; and a gulf opened up between regime and society that was not bridged until the late 1980s when Solidarity was legalised and allowed to contest the parliamentary elections of 1989, when it won an overwhelming victory.

There was no overt challenge to Poland's international alliances during 1980–1, and the Communist Party had nominally retained its leading role. Nor did it necessarily follow that independent trade unions were incompatible with communist rule, as the Yugoslavian experience appeared to demonstrate. But Yugoslavia was not a member of the Warsaw Pact, and it was in an entirely different geostrategic situation – with a much smaller territory and population, in the Balkans and not between Russia and West Germany. The Prague Spring, and later the establishment of Solidarity, had made it clear that there would normally be much stricter limits to the accommodation that could be negotiated between Eastern Europe's communist governments and their often disaffected societies. There could be greater consultation, more respect for the rule of law, greater tolerance for religious believers and more attention to the needs of the domestic consumer. But, until the rules were changed in the late 1980s, there could be no challenge to the ultimate authority of the ruling party, and there could be no challenge to the integrity of the system of alliances that bound together the USSR and its closest allies.

5 A system in decline

By the mid-1980s, when Mikhail Gorbachev became Soviet party leader, there were many who thought communist rule had become firmly established (so, apparently, did he). Partly this was a matter of longevity: there were more and more who had been brought up under socialist conditions, few who had any conscious recollection of a different kind of society. Partly, too, it stemmed from a victory in the Second World War that had been bought at a heavy price, but which appeared to suggest that a system of the Soviet type could overcome the military might of Nazi Germany and do so by rallying ordinary people to its support. Furthermore, it appeared it was a matter of the policies that had been pursued under communist rule, or what it had become conventional to regard as the 'gains of socialism': full employment, cheap housing and transport, low prices for basic foodstuffs. This, some thought, could even be called a communist 'social contract'. There was no opportunity to reject the regime itself; but the regime, by way of compensation, provided a standard of living that was acceptable and steadily improving.

With the benefit of hindsight, it is clear this was an illusory stability. Living standards had been maintained, but at a cost in rising subsidies that could not endlessly be sustained. And yet any attempt to raise prices would prejudice the understanding that had apparently been reached with the wider society. Levels of economic growth had similarly been higher than in the capitalist countries, but they had been steadily slowing, and during the 1970s they became increasingly dependent on the export of oil and gas to Western markets. With slower rates of economic growth, social mobility ossified: there were fewer white-collar jobs for working-class children, and fewer opportunities for all the graduates that flowed out of an expanded higher-education system. With fewer resources, it was less easy to satisfy consumers but at the same time to provide the armed forces with what they needed. And slower growth meant fewer new homes, fewer schools and hospitals, fewer signs that communism was 'on the march' and a system that could inspire the support of working people in other countries.

Central to all of these developments was the falling rate of economic growth; and analysis of it must be central to any adequate account of the decline of a system that had promised to overtake the richest capitalist country by 1970, but which was falling further behind for most of the 1970s and 1980s. Equally, a falling rate of economic growth meant that shortages became more acute, and this meant in turn that the privileges of the party–state leadership became less acceptable to those who were denied them. It was nowhere suggested that socialist societies should be absolutely equal in their distribution of material rewards: it was only in a future communist society that all would be able to satisfy their reasonable requirements. But for some there was already enough evidence of systematic and continuing inequality to justify the identification of a communist ruling group that had most of the distinguishing features of the capitalist ruling class they were supposed to have left behind.

THE ECONOMIC SLOWDOWN

Lenin had claimed that socialism would eventually prevail because its levels of productivity were higher than the social system with which it was in competition. For some time he seemed to be right, particularly in the country that had committed itself for longest to the system he had established. Tsarist Russia had been a backward state, even by the standards of the time. Living standards were low, about 10–15 per cent of the level that had been achieved in Western Europe and North America; and only a quarter of the population could read and write, at a time when literacy was close to universal in the other industrial countries. Seventy years later the contrast could hardly have been greater. The USSR was one of the world's two superpowers, heading one of its largest concentrations of military might. In many areas (like steel and tractors) it led the world, and it had pioneered the exploration of outer space. Soviet industrial production, just 3 per cent of the global total in 1917, had increased to 20 per cent by the late 1980s; the communist-ruled countries among them produced a third of the world's output.

And yet there was deepening evidence as the 1970s advanced that the communist countries had not discovered the secret of high and continuing levels of economic growth. Most obviously, there was a steady fall in reported levels of growth, from 10 per cent or more in the early post-war years to much lower levels by the 1970s and to values that were often negative in the 1980s (see Table 5.1). The targets for industrial output, as a result, were not met in any of the Five-Year Plans after 1970; before that date performance had only once fallen short. Each extra unit of output, moreover, had been bought at the cost of an increasing amount of energy and raw material,

Table 5.1 Economic performance under communist rule, 1951–85 (average annual rates of growth, official data, percentages)

Country	1951–5	1956–60	1961–5	1966–70	1971–5	1976–80	1981–5
Bulgaria	12.2	9.7	6.7	8.8	7.8	6.1	3.7
Czechoslovakia	8.2	7.0	1.9	7.0	5.5	3.7	1.7
GDR	13.1	7.1	3.5	5.2	5.4	4.1	4.5
Hungary	5.7	5.9	4.1	6.8	6.3	2.8	1.3
Poland	8.6	6.6	6.2	6.0	9.8	1.2	−0.8
Romania	14.1	6.6	9.1	7.7	11.4	7.0	4.4
Czechoslovakia	8.2	7.0	1.9	7.0	5.5	3.7	1.7
USSR	11.4	9.2	6.5	7.8	5.7	4.3	3.2
CMEA as a whole	10.8	8.5	6.0	7.4	6.4	4.1	3.0

unlike the experience of the Western nations. And the figures themselves were highly suspect. There was evidence that suggested an increasing level of over-reporting; and official growth rates had also to take into account the increasing tendency to replace perfectly adequate products with equivalents that were very similar but more expensive. Once these factors were included, levels of national income in the USSR had probably stagnated, or even fallen, as early as the late 1970s.

Much of Soviet industrial output was in any case hardly a contribution to real wealth. More tractors and combine harvesters were produced, for instance, than people were available to operate them. More than twice as much steel was produced than in the USA, but there was a smaller output of finished products. More than twice as many pairs of footwear were produced than in the USA, but many more had to be imported as their quality and design were so poor. Even on Soviet official figures some alarming developments were beginning to occur. Soviet national income, for instance, 67 per cent of that of the USA in 1980, had slipped to 64 per cent by 1988, and labour productivity in agriculture, already low, had fallen from 'about 20 per cent' of the US figure in the 1970s to 16 per cent in the late 1980s. The figures for grain production between 1981 and 1986 were so bad that they were simply suppressed.

Several factors were usually blamed for the Soviet economic slow-down, both in the West and in the USSR itself. One reason, certainly, was that the increase in the size of the industrial labour force was levelling off. Throughout the 1950s and 1960s large numbers of people were leaving the land to work in industry, allowing output to increase through additional labour inputs rather than through higher productivity. By the early 1980s this outflow had largely come to an end, leaving industrial growth much more dependent upon an increase in the efficiency with which existing resources were used. The population had also been ageing, which meant that, as in many Western countries, a relatively smaller labour force was required to support a relatively larger group of pensioners and other members of the non-working population (known as the 'dependency ratio'). Some 7 per cent of the Soviet population was aged 60 or over in 1939; by 1987 the proportion had doubled to 14 per cent, and by the year 2000, according to Soviet demographers, the proportion of the elderly could be expected to increase still further, to 17–18 per cent.

A further contribution to the economic slowdown came from the fact that raw materials which were conveniently located and of the required high quality had gradually been used up, making it increasingly necessary to extract resources from more remote locations and poorer sources of supply. Additional resources of this kind were increasingly costly per unit of production as they required additional expenditure on extraction, refinement and transportation. In the 1960s, it has been calculated, one rouble of production in the extractive industries required two roubles of investment; by the early 1980s the same level of output required seven roubles. More attention had also to be paid to quality and design if goods were to find buyers in an increasingly demanding market, and to such 'externalities' as environmental conservation, which tended to raise unit costs still further. Very poor levels of agricultural production in the late 1970s and early 1980s, caused to a large extent by adverse weather conditions, made a further contribution to reduced levels of economic growth during these years.

It was none the less clear, whatever the circumstances involved, that a steadily falling rate of economic growth could not be sustained without serious damage to the international standing of the USSR, and to the 'social contract' between regime and society. Gorbachev and two other speakers warned the 27th Party Congress in 1986 that even the political stability of the USSR could not be taken for granted if popular expectations of this kind continued to be disappointed. As Gorbachev had put it in a speech in December 1984 shortly before he became party leader, only a highly developed economy would allow the USSR to enter the twenty-first century as a great and flourishing power; the fate of socialism as a whole, not just in the USSR, depended upon the success of their efforts. Other commentators argued, in still more apocalyptic terms, that unless the USSR achieved more efficient forms of economic management it would cease to be a great power and would enter the new century as a 'backward, stagnating state and an example to the rest of the world how not to conduct its economic life' (in the words of Nikolai Shmelev, a prominent reform economist, in 1988).

The same tendencies, moreover, were apparent in the countries of Eastern Europe. In Poland, for instance, the system of state ownership and planning that had been established under communist rule helped to bring about a recovery after the devastation of the Second World War and transformed a predominantly agrarian country into an industrial power. But, as elsewhere in the region, there were characteristic weaknesses. Low levels of productivity persisted in agriculture, which remained in largely private hands. There was an overconcentration on heavy industry and the needs of the defence economy, at the expense of consumers; and real wages stagnated. The failure to improve living standards lay behind the disturbances that took place in the Baltic ports in 1970, which led to the fall of the Gomułka leadership. The strategy that was followed by the new leadership of Edward Gierek allowed real wages to rise rapidly in the early 1970s, but prices were kept down by an increasingly heavy burden of subsidy and foreign debt, and some kind of adjustment could hardly be avoided. The outcome, as we saw in Chapter 4, was a further attempt to raise prices in 1980 and still more determined resistance from ordinary workers, now organised in Solidarity.

Polish economic development was also accompanied by a steady deterioration in the social infrastructure and natural environment. The housing stock became increasingly dilapidated; hospitals were frequently short of the equipment and medicines they required; and there were periodic power cuts. Environmental pollution, meanwhile, became a steadily more serious threat to human survival. Poland was still highly dependent on coal for its energy supply. For this and other reasons, half of the country's water by the late 1980s was unusable, and only 1 per cent was suitable for drinking. There were direct consequences for health – with sharp increases in childhood leukaemia and other serious illnesses – and for agriculture – with for instance a quarter of the land around Krakow so poisoned by chemicals and metals that its produce was unfit for human consumption. Polish industry in the coastal areas also made its contribution to the ecological degradation of the Baltic Sea.

For all the variations from country to country, communist economies had a number of common and apparently systemic weaknesses. They were effective, clearly, in performing straightforward tasks that had well defined objectives: building a railway system, eliminating illiteracy, winning a war. But as communist economies moved from 'extensive' to the more complicated tasks of 'intensive' growth, based on higher levels of productivity, their centralised forms of management became a block to further development. Central planning, for a start, meant that the preferences of planners, not those of consumers, were dominant. So less attention was paid to what mattered to ordinary people, like quality and design, and rather more to the requirements of the military-industrial complex, transport and construction, which had powerful advocates in government. There was little incentive to innovate, because rewards were tied to plan fulfilment and a risky initiative might not pay off. Enterprises, in any case, were often monopoly producers, not just in their own country but across the region, so there was no domestic competition to drive up performance, and there was no need to worry (because they were publicly owned) about going bankrupt if there was no demand for what they sold.

Nor was there any foreign competition, because access to the domestic market was closely regulated and few Western companies wanted a currency that could not be converted back into their own. Workers, for their part, had few incentives: wage differentials were very narrow, and at the same time it was rare to be fired for poor performance. A Western visitor to a Polish factory, supposedly, asked how many people worked there; he was told 'about half of them'. Prices, moreover, were artificial; they were heavily subsidised, particularly in the case of foodstuffs, and could often be less than the cost of production. So bread was fed to livestock, because it was cheaper than grain; and as more was consumed at these low prices the more the burden of subsidies increased. There were, of course, all kinds of attempts to deal with these problems from the 1960s onwards, but it had not been found possible, up to the end of communist rule, to combine the strengths of central planning with the incentives that were provided by market mechanisms.

A STRATIFYING SOCIETY

A slowing rate of economic growth had serious implications for East European societies. With industry rapidly expanding, there were more opportunities for white-collar employment – in management, ministries and research bureaux. A rising national income made it possible to increase enrolments at all levels of the educational system, particularly in universities and colleges, and at the same time to improve pensions and other social benefits. The special needs of women and mothers could be given more attention, while at the same time attending to working conditions in construction and the mines. The interests of the armed forces could be satisfied at the same time as those of consumers – there could be guns as well as butter. And there could be a serious attempt to bring the level of development in poorer regions up to the levels of more affluent, industrially developed and urban areas.

Higher enrolments in universities and colleges meant a larger pool of recruits for managerial and administrative positions, drawn from a wider cross-section of the society. But war and post-war reconstruction had created unusual opportunities for career advancement, and as growth slowed down and upward advancement became more difficult, it was clear that social differences were beginning to reproduce themselves. Equally, the communist states were acquiring some of the characteristics of the patterns of stratification of their capitalist counterparts. The increasingly significant differences in income meant real and observable differences in lifestyle. More affluent Hungarians, for instance, spent three times as much as the average on newspapers, eight times as much on going to the theatre and thirty-three times as much on books. They had a different diet as well: they ate less cabbage and bread, but more mushrooms and asparagus. Similarly, they spent more on cosmetics and domestic assistance, and on their health care.

There was a further convergence in the prestige of various occupations in East and West. In Poland, for instance, the hierarchy ran from professionals, technicians and foremen to skilled, office and service workers, craftsmen, unskilled workers, and finally to farmers and farm labourers. Throughout the region the upper-professional occupations stood out as being consistently high in desirability and popular regard, with unskilled jobs, manual and non-manual, at the other extreme. In East and West, again, there was a tendency for women to have less well-paid and well-regarded jobs, with a concentration in certain occupations and at lower levels of skill and responsibility; the same was true of members of ethnic minorities.

What mattered still more was that these differences were becoming more firmly established as the dislocation of purges, war and post-war reconstruction was succeeded by more stable conditions. Marriages were overwhelmingly to partners from the same social group (in the USSR 87 per cent of peasant men chose wives from the same social category, and in Hungary 97 per cent). Similarly, husbands and wives were very likely to have the same level of education; and the same was true of social circles, with up to three-quarters of the members of various social strata likely to choose their friends from the same category. There was a strong relationship, in turn, between the educational attainment of children and of their parents. Children of parents with a university or college degree, for instance, did much better at school than the children of parents with a less advanced education. Home background also influenced the age at which children left school: more children from professional families continued into the later classes at school, and fewer dropped out while at university or college. A Hungarian study found that 83 per cent of the children of upper professionals remained at school after the compulsory attending age, but that (at the other extreme) only 15 per cent of the children of unskilled workers did so.

Not surprisingly, there were some who argued that a socialist society of this kind was qualitatively no different from capitalism; specifically, that its ruling group was the functional equivalent of a capitalist ruling class. The strongest formulations of this kind came from Yugoslavia, and from its political leadership. Edvard Kardelj, for instance, chairman of the Yugoslavian parliament and the regime's leading theorist, rejected Western liberal or 'bourgeois' democracy, but he also rejected bureaucratic state socialism, the 'socialism of the apparat' that prevailed throughout the bloc. Yugoslavian socialism was based on rather different principles – direct democracy and workers' self-government; and these principles, Kardelj suggested, were reflected in the Yugoslavian system of workers' councils that had been established after 1950. Kardelj, and Tito himself, took their inspiration from Marx's and Lenin's writings on the radical democracy that had prevailed in the Paris Commune of 1870–1, and claimed that in Yugoslavia itself the state was beginning to 'wither away' in the way that classical theory had indicated.

Another of the regime's leading figures, Tito's friend and close associate Milovan Djilas, went much further. Djilas had found himself at odds with the Soviet leadership as early as 1944, and then took the lead in the struggle against Stalinism in his own country. By 1953, however, he was beginning to demand more than the right to construct a Yugoslavian road to socialism, declaring that the Leninist type of party and state was obsolete and condemning the selfishness and incompetence of the new ruling group. Djilas was obliged to surrender all his party and state posts, and was then sentenced to a number of years in prison for having published articles in the foreign press that were critical of the communist system. While Djilas was serving his term in prison his book *The New Class* appeared in the West, in 1957; he was given another seven years for transmitting this book abroad and for his anti-communist activities, and was released in 1961 on condition that he keep out of politics. He was arrested again the following year and sentenced to five years for publishing his *Conversations with Stalin* in the West, but was pardoned in 1966. He remained a thorn in the flesh of his more orthodox colleagues up to his death in 1995.

Communist systems, for Djilas, were state capitalist, not socialist, and they were dominated by a professional party bureaucracy, not by working people. The bureaucracy, he argued, had a 'special privileged position' in these societies, which arose from their monopoly of the allocation of rewards. Nominally, the ownership of wealth was in the hands of ordinary people, but in practical terms ownership meant the rights to control and to enjoy the benefits of possession, and these were firmly in the hands of party and state officials. The development of the communist states, Djilas suggested, had seen the origin of a new form of ownership, and of a new ruling and exploiting class; and the revolutions that had been conducted in the name of communist ideas, supposedly to abolish class itself, had resulted in the total dominance of a 'new class of owners and exploiters'.

The new class was, in effect, the party-state bureaucracy; it could be defined as the members of a given society who enjoyed privilege and material advantage because of the administrative position they occupied. There were enormous differences in income between officials and ordinary workers, and there was a 'special type of corruption' caused by the fact that government was in the hands of a single political group, which was the source of all privileges. Things were no different, in substance, in Yugoslavia, in spite of its 'so-called workers' management and autonomy'. There had been no increase in the share of profits that went to those who produced, either nationally or at the level of individual enterprises; the establishment of the system had been a partial concession to popular pressure, but taxes took away the profits that workers believed they had won for themselves, leaving them with 'crumbs from the table and illusions'.

An older but still more influential statement of the 'bureaucratic degeneration' thesis was that of Leon Trotsky, particularly in his *Revolution Betrayed* of 1937. Trotsky argued that the USSR was still a proletarian or socialist state because it was one in which land, industry and the other means of production had been taken into public ownership. The productive resources of the society, however, were not being used for the benefit of all its members because the bureaucracy, the 'sole privileged and commanding stratum in Soviet society', had taken control of the state machinery and was using that control to further its own selfish interests. The means of production still belonged to the state, which, in turn, 'belonged' to the bureaucracy, which had 'expropriated the proletariat politically'. If the bureaucracy succeeded in making its position a more permanent and legally based one, particularly through the creation of special forms of private property, the gains of the October revolution would eventually be liquidated. The revolution, however, had been betrayed but not yet overthrown, and it might still be redeemed by a 'supplementary revolution' in which the working class would seize political power back from the bureaucracy.

Theories of this kind were clearly relevant to the patterns of inequality that had persisted after a revolution that was supposed to eliminate the basis for their existence. But they were open themselves to a number of serious objections. Initially, they were generally rather vague about the nature and composition of 'the bureaucracy' that was so central to their accounts. Should it be defined, for instance, in terms of income (but then many writers, musicians and scientists would have to be included) or in terms of position (but many who enjoyed a substantial degree of political power did not necessarily enjoy a comparable degree of material advantage)? How large was 'the bureaucracy', and how did it cohere as a social group in the absence of special 'ruling class' educational and other institutions?

Second, and more importantly, how did 'the bureaucracy' reproduce itself? Given the absence of private ownership of productive wealth, a ruling group in the communist countries, however defined, could not transfer a position of guaranteed material advantage to its descendants, as a ruling group could do in a capitalist society. Certainly, something could be achieved through personal connections, and particularly through privileged access to higher education. It was none the less striking how few members of this 'sole privileged and commanding stratum' were succeeded to their positions of political power as well as social advantage by their children or close relatives. 'Privileges', as Trotsky had pointed out, 'have only half their value if they cannot be transmitted to one's children', and for this reason he thought it was 'inevitable' that the bureaucracy would seek a more enduring form of advantage such as that provided by private property. For writers in the Trotskyist tradition, this was precisely what the 'transition' was all about: the communist ruling group using their political influence to secure a disproportionate share of the state property that was passing at this point into private ownership.

Material inequalities, such as special shops and hospital facilities, were in any case no evidence of exploitation in a Marxist sense. For this to apply, it would be necessary to show that one class regularly appropriated the surplus value produced by another, the exploited or subordinate class. Marx, however, defined classes in terms of their relationship to the means of production, and there was no private ownership of such resources in the communist countries that could provide a basis for the appropriation of surplus value in the manner he had indicated. The fact that workers produced more than they directly consumed was no more conclusive evidence of exploitation, given the need for reinvestment, defence and administration, and for the redistribution of resources towards the old, the sick and the very young. Indeed, for writers like Fehér, Heller and Márkus in their *Dictatorship over Needs* (1983), the communist countries were better analysed as a new and quite specific social formation that had little in common with either socialism or capitalism, and in which it was political power that gave access to economic advantage, not the other way round.

The privileges of ruling groups in the communist world were, perhaps surprisingly, often modest. All kinds of groups had their occupational advantages: scientists, writers and sportsmen as well as party functionaries. And all of them had their holiday homes, their special shops, their residential areas and their private restaurants. But, understandably, the privileges of the party functionaries emerged as a public issue in the late 1980s, as the press began to report them more openly and as the economic difficulties of ordinary people made them more difficult to tolerate; and it was one of Boris Yeltsin's most effective slogans as he campaigned against the Soviet party authorities. There was perhaps a certain irony in the way that communist governments lost their position because of their failure to live up to their own ideal of (eventually) a classless society; it was certainly a damaging charge that a relatively small elite seemed to have achieved communism for themselves and not necessarily for their long-suffering fellow citizens.

6   Transition from below

Political change in the communist world at the end of the 1980s took a variety of forms, reflecting a range of internal and external factors. There was, however, a relatively clear distinction between the regimes that were overthrown 'from below' by popular action (in Poland, for instance, or in Czechoslovakia) and those in which the regime itself initiated change 'from above' and in some cases retained power (as in Hungary or Bulgaria). The central drama took place during the *annus mirabilis* of 1989, when a series of interconnected changes swept across Central and Eastern Europe; but there were no changes of a comparable kind in the USSR until 1991, and there was no comprehensive change of leadership in Romania until 1996. Equally, there were several countries where communist rule remained intact, most notably in China; the response of the authorities there to the pressure of a student movement for democratic change was to order tanks to suppress their unarmed demonstration on Tianenmen Square in June 1989, prompting some discussion of a 'Chinese model' that combined economic liberalism with political authoritarianism.

Albania, to take a Balkan example, was a relatively clear case of political change 'from below'. The ruling Party of Labour rode out the storm of 1989 and appeared to have secured its position by an overwhelming victory at the parliamentary elections that took place in March 1991. But continuing demonstrations and a general strike led to another election in March 1992 at which it was comprehensively defeated by a newly formed Democratic Party. The Party of Labour renamed itself the Socialist Party and repudiated its former ideology, and a year later the collected works of Enver Hoxha, party leader until 1985, were being turned into cardboard boxes; later still, in 1997, Albania was one of the countries that voted the former communists back into power, after their successors had proved no more successful in dealing with the country's economic problems. There was a more varied picture in neighbouring Yugoslavia, which began to dissolve into its constituent republics after 1991. In Slovenia, a former communist retained the presidency after a peaceful change of regime; but in the largest of the republics, Serbia, the former communists won presidential as well as parliamentary elections on a broadly nationalist platform that led directly to the subordination of the autonomous province of Kosovo and an international conflict in the spring of 1999. There was still, nominally, a Yugoslavia; but in substance it was one of the four states that did not survive the transition, along with Czechoslovakia, the German Democratic Republic and the USSR.

THE TRANSITION IN POLAND AND THE GDR

Perhaps the clearest case of political change 'from below' was in Poland, where communist rule had always been resisted because it was Russian and not just because it was Marxist, and where the experience of Solidarity in 1980–1 had convinced most Poles that, as Adam Michnik put it, there was no prospect of a 'socialism with a human face'; what remained was 'communism with its teeth knocked out'. A number of attempts were made to establish a dialogue with society after Solidarity had been suspended and then banned: a national public opinion centre was established in 1982, martial law was lifted a year later, and the regime committed itself to a programme of 'socialist renewal' that in many ways anticipated the reforms that were conducted in the USSR under the Gorbachev leadership. An attempt to secure popular endorsement in November 1987, however, came badly unstuck when a referendum failed to secure the necessary majority of the electorate – although there was a majority of voters – for the government's proposals for economic and social change. A wave of strikes broke out in April 1988 and again in August, which were only brought to an end by the promise of negotiations between the authorities, the Catholic Church and representatives of Solidarity. Talks began – around a very large round table – in February 1989, and by April an agreement had been reached that included the legalisation of Solidarity and the holding of elections to a new two-chamber parliament. It was an agreement that had enormous implications for the entire region.

Under the terms of the April agreement, Solidarity would be allowed to resume its activities and it would receive airtime on radio and television as well as its own national and regional newspapers. There would also be new parliamentary elections at which the Solidarity-led opposition would be allowed to compete for 35 per cent of the seats in the restructured lower house, the Sejm. Even more far-reaching was the reconstitution of a second legislative chamber, the Senate, for which elections were to be completely free and open. At the signing ceremony the Solidarity leader, Lech Wałęsa, declared 'this is the beginning of democracy and a free Poland'; as it turned out, this was scarcely an exaggeration.

Under the terms of the round-table agreement, the opposition would be allowed to contest 161 of the 460 seats in the Sejm and all 100 seats in the new Senate. In the Sejm the United Workers' Party reserved 38 per cent of the seats for itself, the balance (27 per cent) going to its allied parties in the government. The Solidarity-led opposition was at a great disadvantage in that it had just two months to transform itself from an illegal underground organisation into a national political presence. The governing parties, however, ran a confused and badly organised campaign, and dissipated their limited resources by fielding several candidates in their allotted constituencies.

The first round of voting on 4 June produced an almost complete victory for the Solidarity-led opposition, with straight wins in 92 of the 100 seats in the Senate and in 160 of the 161 seats for which they could compete in the Sejm. There was a further humiliation for the communist authorities in the separate election that took place for a national list, in that only 2 of the 35 candidates they had sponsored were able to secure the necessary 50 per cent of the votes cast (the defeated candidates included several ministers and Politburo members). In the second round of voting on 18 June the Solidarity alliance won a further seat in the Sejm – which meant that it had won all the seats it could contest in that chamber – and seven of the eight remaining Senate seats – which meant that it had won 99 of the 100 seats in the upper house (the other went to an independent). Solidarity had 161 seats in the Sejm against the 173 held by the United Workers' Party, but its overwhelming success in the seats that could be freely contested was a shattering blow to the communist authorities. On these results, Solidarity could speak for about 65 per cent of those who had voted, or about 40 per cent of the entire electorate, and it very quickly became the dominant force in Polish politics.

In line with the round-table agreement the communist leader, General Jaruzelski, won the presidency when the new parliament assembled, but by a single vote. Attempts to form a communist-led government were less successful, and in August 1989 a new administration was formed under the leadership of Tadeusz Mazowiecki, a Catholic intellectual who had formerly edited Solidarity's weekly paper, with communist ministers left in charge of defence and internal security. Outlining his government's programme to the Sejm on 12 September, Mazowiecki promised to turn Poland into a 'sovereign, democratic state based on the rule of law' that would be 'open to Europe and the world' and would contribute to the dissolution of the two military blocs.

There were more particular plans for the economy, under the guidance of Deputy Prime Minister Leszek Balcerowicz. His strategy became known as 'shock therapy', and it went into almost immediate effect. The longer-term objective was a transformation of the economy through the privatisation of state industry, the creation of capital markets, a convertible currency and a shift away from heavy industry towards consumer goods. Virtually all price controls were lifted and most government subsidies were eliminated, forcing the companies concerned to become profitable or go out of business. The elimination of subsidies helped to reduce the budget deficit and to reverse the growth of foreign debt. There were also to be anti-inflation measures, including restrictions on wage increases, reductions in the money supply and sharp increases in interest rates to restrain credit demand and stimulate savings. A parallel programme of privatisation was to begin with smaller enterprises; a programme for the privatisation of larger-scale enterprises was announced in the summer of 1991. National income fell by 12 per cent in 1990, inflation remained stubbornly high and unemployment started to increase; but, as reformers liked to remark, you couldn't cross a precipice in two jumps.

There were further changes in public life. The armed forces were depoliticised, a regular police force was brought into being, and the much-hated riot police were replaced by regionally based public order groups. The secret police had its functions taken over by a state security bureau; all members of the judiciary and procuracy were vetted and considerable numbers were not reappointed, although the round-table agreement had included a provision that there would be no victimisation of the officials who had served in the previous regime. Later in the year the Polish People's Republic became the Polish Republic, sovereignty was transferred from the 'working people of town and country' to 'the nation', and the reference to the leading role of the Workers' Party was removed from the constitution, which now defined Poland as a 'law-based state implementing the principle of social justice'. The crown was restored to the head of the white eagle in the national coat of arms, and in a further change of symbols the communist National Day (22 July) was replaced by the more traditional 3 May.

It was crucial to these developments that the Soviet leadership had been prepared to accept them without apparent concern. As *Izvestiya* noted, the Workers' Party would 'incidentally, no longer have a majority' in the Polish parliament; the Soviet government, for its part, congratulated Mazowiecki on his new responsibilities and noted that he intended to maintain Poland's international alliances. It was none the less Eastern Europe's first non-communist government for more than forty years, and a clear breach of the power monopoly that had been established after the Second World War. The Workers' Party meanwhile reconstituted itself as the Social Democracy of the Polish Republic and elected Alexander Kwasniewski, a former sports and youth minister, as its chairman. Lech Wałęsa was re-elected chairman of Solidarity itself in April 1990 with 78 per cent of the vote; in September Jaruzelski stepped down, and at the election that took place in November Wałęsa became Poland's first non-communist president.

The process of political change 'from below' took still more dramatic forms in the German Democratic Republic, which was a special case in that it was a political construct rather than a nation-state. The transition began in the summer of 1989 with an outflow of population through Hungary to West Germany, and developed into a widespread resistance movement led by the Lutheran Church and an oppositional coalition known as New Forum. Party leader Erich Honecker had been in hospital during the year, but he apparently believed there was no need to contemplate far-reaching change, and publicly supported the suppression of the Tiananmen Square demonstration in China. As another member of the GDR leadership had memorably remarked, 'just because your neighbour changes his wallpaper is no reason to change your own'. The fortieth anniversary of the GDR was celebrated with appropriate pomp in October 1989, in the presence of Mikhail Gorbachev, who congratulated the East Germans on their successes, although he also warned that 'he who comes too late is punished by life'.

Mounting public pressure led other members of the leadership to agree that Honecker would have to step down, and he was forced to resign shortly after the anniversary celebrations. But the demonstrations continued, with hundreds of thousands appearing weekly on the streets of Leipzig and even more in East Berlin. In early November the government and the entire Politburo resigned. Further concessions followed, including an announcement that citizens of the GDR would be allowed to travel to other countries with the minimum of formalities; the result was a rush to the border crossings along the Berlin Wall on the night of 9 November 1989. The ruling Socialist Union Party changed its name to the Party of Democratic Socialism, and elected a new leader. The new leadership announced that multi-party elections would take place the following year; at those elections, in March 1990, the conservative Christian Democratic Union took the largest share of the vote and began to move rapidly towards union with the Federal Republic. A treaty of unification was signed on 31 August, and at midnight on 2 October 1990 the German Democratic Republic disappeared into a reunified German state under the Christian Democratic government of Helmut Kohl.

THE TRANSITION IN ROMANIA AND CZECHOSLOVAKIA

The most spectacular case of political change 'from below' was in Romania, although it was less clear that there had been a decisive break with communist rule – or at any rate, with the people and institutions that had ruled the country in the recent past. Nicolae Ceauşescu had been party leader and virtual dictator of Romania since 1965. The centre of a bizarre personality cult, he had been declared a 'genius of the Carpathians', a 'Danube of Thought', and the 'Chosen One'; his home village became a place of pilgrimage (in 1976 the earliest traces of *homo sapiens* were 'discovered' nearby), and on his sixty-second birthday in 1982 he was declared divine. His wife Elena was a first deputy prime minister and a member of the party leadership; his son was first secretary in Transylvania and a candidate member of the leadership, and other relatives were in key ministerial or diplomatic positions (this was sometimes called 'socialism in a single family'). As late as November 1989 there was little obvious threat to Ceauşescu at the Romanian Communist Party's 14th Congress, officially dubbed a 'Congress of the Great Socialist Victory'; the leader's own six-hour speech was interrupted by no fewer than 125 standing ovations (these owed something to the man in the control room who switched on pre-recorded applause at the appropriate moments), and the resolutions that were adopted showed little sign of compromise. The regime, in any case, could dispose of a security police, the Securitate, that operated wherever necessary outside the framework of the law and indeed beyond national boundaries.

The fall of the regime began shortly afterwards, with demonstrations in the largely Hungarian city of Timişoara, which were crushed with exceptional ferocity. The protest none the less spread to other towns and cities and to the capital Bucharest, where Ceauşescu, addressing a public rally on 21 December, was ignominiously shouted down. The following day he fled the capital in a helicoptor so overloaded that one of the crew had to sit in his lap, but he was captured shortly afterwards and brought to trial after further street-fighting had claimed thousands of lives. On 25 December Ceauşescu and his wife were put on trial, sentenced to death for 'genocide' and summarily executed; reports began to circulate at the same time of the extraordinary opulence in which the former dictator had lived, including a house crammed with art treasures and a nuclear bunker lined with marble. The functions of government were carried on, after Ceauşescu's overthrow, by the National Salvation Front, a coalition within which former communists were in a commanding position. At the multi-party elections that took place in May 1990 the Front and its presidential candidate, Ion Iliescu, won convincing victories; Iliescu, a former Politburo member, won again in 1992. Arguably, the personal dictatorship of Ceauşescu had ended but the regime itself had continued.

The process of change in Czechoslovakia was more peaceful, but it was also initiated from below against a regime that showed little sign of flexibility after the democratic and socialist objectives of the 'Prague Spring' had been suppressed by the country's Warsaw Pact allies. Gustáv Husák, appointed Dubček's successor as party leader in April 1969, had not been involved in the call for intervention, but he accepted the Soviet view that socialism itself had been threatened by 'counter-revolutionary forces' and that their defeat required the 'restoration of Marxist–Leninist principles in the policy of the party and in the activities of the state'. Reformers were purged from the Communist Party, which lost about a third of its membership, and from other positions of influence; Dubček became a woodcutter, others became taxi-drivers or nightwatchmen. Others still 'adapted', like the manager of a shop in a celebrated essay by Václav Havel who simply put the slogan 'Workers of the world, unite!' alongside the fruit and vegetables in his front window. At the same time there were signs of intellectual dissent with the publication of a manifesto by Charter 77, a loose grouping of campaigners 'for the respect of civil and human rights in our own country and throughout the world'; and a Committee for the Defence of the Unjustly Prosecuted was founded the following year.

The election of Mikhail Gorbachev as CPSU General Secretary confronted the Czech leaders with a serious dilemma. They had always quoted the USSR as their ideal, but they could hardly adopt the reforming policies its leadership was now pursuing without conceding that their own policies had been mistaken for nearly twenty years, and perhaps prejudicing their position. In the end they compromised. A more modest version of perestroika was approved in 1987, involving a greater degree of factory self-management and financial accountability; at the same time party and government leaders continued to repudiate the Prague Spring and to insist, as Husák put it, that they were 'looking for their own solutions' and not simply following the reforms that were taking place in the USSR, in which their own people were showing a close interest (Gorbachev himself had a very warm reception when he paid a visit in April 1987). There was also some leadership change: Husák remained president, a post he had assumed in 1975, but the party first secretaryship went to Mílos Jakes in December 1987. Jakes had been directly responsible for the purging of reformists from party ranks after 1968 and his appointment was a sign that the regime might be prepared to consider economic reform in response to falling growth rates but that there would be no political liberalisation.

The following year saw a deepening disenchantment, set against a background of worsening shortages. There was public pressure for a greater degree of religious tolerance, particularly in Slovakia, and a petition in favour of religious freedom, initiated by the Archbishop of Prague, attracted almost 600,000 signatures. But there was still more substantial pressure for political reform. In August 1988, 10,000 demonstrated on the twentieth anniversary of the Warsaw Pact invasion. Several thousand rallied once again on 28 October, which was the seventieth anniversary of the foundation of the state, and thousands more on 10 December, the fortieth anniversary of the Universal Declaration of Human Rights. And then for several days in January 1989 thousands gathered at the spot in Prague's Wenceslas Square where student Jan Palach had set himself alight in 1969 to protest against the invasion the previous year; the police had to use batons, dogs and tear gas to disperse the demonstrators, and dozens were arrested. A national appeal, 'Just a few sentences', appeared in June calling for more far-reaching democratisation and the opening of a dialogue between the authorities and the society; within a month it had attracted 10,000 signatures; by September there were 40,000.

The eruption of demonstrations in November 1989 was none the less a surprise to most observers, as well as to the party leadership. Inspired by the success of oppositionists in Poland and East Germany and by the evidence that the 'Brezhnev Doctrine' was no longer valid, students in Prague took the opportunity of an officially sponsored demonstration on 17 November, organised to honour student victims of the Nazis fifty years earlier, to demand more radical changes, including 'genuine perestroika' and 'free elections'. As many as 15,000 took part, more than had been expected, and the brutality of the police response – at least 150 were injured – led to a widening public protest, initially among intellectuals in the main cities, and then throughout the wider public. An umbrella organisation, Civic Forum, was set up on 19 November to coordinate opposition protests, led by the playwright and founder of Charter 77 Václav Havel, and dedicated to the achievement of a 'legal, democratic state in the spirit of the traditions of Czech statehood and of the international principles expressed in the Universal Declaration of Human Rights and the International Covenant on Civil and Political Rights'; its Slovak counterpart was called Public against Violence. Faced by this mounting tide of popular dissatisfaction Jakes and the entire party leadership were obliged to resign at a stormy Central Committee meeting that took place on 24 and 25 November, and there were promises that there would be freedom of travel, a new press law and competitive elections.

Events, however, had acquired their own momentum. Three-quarters of a million (5 per cent of the country's population) demonstrated on Letna Plain in Prague on 25 and 26 November and there was a general strike the following day in which half the country was reported to have taken part. The Federal Assembly, meanwhile, voted to remove the leading role of the Communist Party from the constitution and withdrew its condemnation of the Prague Spring. A new coalition government was formed on 3 December with five non-communist members, but it was unable to generate public confidence and resigned four days later. On 10 December President Husák swore in a 'government of national understanding' and himself resigned. The new government was headed by Marián Čalfa, a Slovak reform communist, but it had a non-communist majority; it was to hold office, in any event, only until new parliamentary elections could take place. On 28 December Alexander Dubček, the hero of 1968, was elected speaker of parliament, and on

29 December Václav Havel, under arrest at the start of the year, was unanimously elected president. Their first task was to arrange for the elections, which took place in June 1990 and at which Civic Forum took about half the vote in the Czech lands and Public against Violence about a third in Slovakia. It had been a quick but civilised change of regime and it became known as the 'Velvet Revolution'.

7   Transition from above

The end of communist rule was often the result of 'people power', as in Czechoslovakia; but there were also changes 'from above', initiated by the regime itself (or at least by sections of its leadership). They were operating, admittedly, within a constrained environment. As Gorbachev had told his wife on the eve of his assumption of power, 'We can't go on like this'; and this was a view widely shared by party reformers throughout the region. The changes that took place in the USSR were indeed a model of change for many of them. Socialism, they could argue, had secured its position internationally, and at home its collectivist, welfarist values were widely shared. But its forms of government had lagged behind a changing society. Why, for instance, did socialism have to mean single-party rule? The USSR had begun its existence as a coalition of Bolsheviks and Left Socialist Revolutionaries; only an attack on Lenin, in the summer of 1918, had brought it to an end. Then Stalinism had imposed a form of central control that reformers were increasingly willing to call totalitarian. Why not allow a public life to re-emerge within the framework of law, with its destinies determined by the ballot box rather than party directives?

These, clearly, were large assumptions; but at the time they did not appear to be entirely unrealistic. If the survey evidence was any guide, there was a strong popular commitment to the principles of Soviet-style socialism: full employment, comprehensive welfare, and a central role for the state in assuring social progress. And there was strong support for the kinds of change that were being contemplated by reforming leaderships: more openness in the media, a stronger rule of law, a real choice of candidate at elections. This, in fact, might be the only way to sustain communist rule in the longer term. And it was more than a question of the struggle for influence between reformers and their opponents in each of the countries concerned. The USSR itself could influence the process of change elsewhere, partly by abandoning the 'Brezhnev Doctrine', but also by encouraging or even assisting domestic reformers against hard-liners like Ceauşescu and Honecker. Its own transition, which had begun with the democratisation of political life under Gorbachev and then went further after the end of communist rule in 1991, was central to the process.

THE TRANSITION IN BULGARIA AND HUNGARY

In Bulgaria party reformers led the way, encouraged by the democratising changes that Gorbachev had been promoting in the USSR. Unlike Poland or the Baltic, there was no particular hostility towards the USSR and the political principles it represented. Russia had freed Bulgaria from Turkish rule in the 1870s, within generous boundaries; a statue of Alexander II stood in the main square of its capital, erected by a grateful people. Indeed, there were plans after the war to incorporate Bulgaria as one of the republics of the USSR; the two countries, as party leader Todor Zhivkov put it, had a 'single circulatory system'. Zhivkov, who had been in power since 1954, set the process of reform in motion with a speech in July 1987 that called for a shift from 'power in the name of the people to power by means of the people' and for a 'self-managing society'. The changes became known as the 'July Concept'; later, in 1988, Zhivkov developed them into a Bulgarian version of perestroika.

The reforms, however, were implemented without conviction, and Zhivkov himself became increasingly arbitrary and corrupt. His speeches and writings appeared in large editions, prompting locals to remark that he was the 'only man who had ever written more books than he had read'; his drunken son was appointed to a senior position in the party apparatus. Dissidents, including a developing environmental movement, were treated harshly, and two potential rivals were forced out of office and expelled from the party in July 1988. The economic situation, moreover, was darkening. As elsewhere, growth rates were falling and foreign debt was mounting. Export earnings were hit by the fall in oil prices in the late 1980s (Bulgaria had been earning foreign currency by processing Soviet oil); the USSR, at the same time, began to press for a reduction in its trade deficit and indeed for repayment of the debts of earlier years. Shortages of consumer goods became widespread during 1989, weakening the position of a leadership that was already out of step with its Soviet neighbour; and there were labour shortages arising from the forced repatriation of many of the country's ethnic Turkish minority.

There were public demonstrations against the regime in October and again in early November 1989, which were the largest the country had experienced since the end of the Second World War. But Zhivkov's fall from power shortly afterwards was less the result of pressure of this kind than of the judgement of his party colleagues, in a close vote in the Politburo on 9 November, that he had become a threat to their collective survival. The new party leader was Petar Mladenov, who had been foreign minister since 1971 and apparently enjoyed Moscow's confidence. Under his guidance the party expelled Zhivkov and his son for 'serious violations of basic party and moral principles' and went on to condemn the 'dictatorship of a clan' that they had established. A new party programme, adopted in February 1990, committed the party to 'democratic socialism' in Bulgaria, and to 'democratic and free elections' at the earliest opportunity; the party itself was renamed the Bulgarian Socialist Party, with a red rose rather than a hammer and sickle as its symbol. The party also adopted a new statute that affirmed the right to form factions and to express dissenting opinion within the party; workplace cells were wound up; elections to party office were to take place through a secret and competitive ballot, and for a limited term. The party daily, meanwhile, dropped the historic slogan 'Workers of the world, unite' from its front page.

Political opposition had been legalised by the new regime, and the more important groups entered into a coalition – the Union of Democratic Forces, led by dissident sociologist Zheliu Zhelev – at the end of 1989. The UDF quickly showed its support by organising mass demonstrations in the capital, and its leaders gained the agreement of the communists to enter into round-table discussions on the future of the country. The round table, which functioned as a substitute parliament, reached decisions on three basic issues. The first provided for the election of a Grand National Assembly of 400 deputies, half elected by single-member constituencies and half by proportional representation. The GNA was expected in its turn to function as a constituent assembly as well as a parliament, and to design a new political structure for the country. A neutral commission whose membership was approved by both sides was set up to implement the election agreement. The round table banned the formation of political parties on an ethnic or religious basis, a measure aimed at preventing the organisation of a separate and perhaps separatist party to represent Bulgaria's Turks and Muslims.

An agreement was reached at the end of March that provided for elections to a new parliament, which would approve a new constitution. At those elections, in June 1990, the former communists campaigned as the Bulgarian Socialist Party, emphasising their experience, their role in ousting Zhivkov and their gradual approach to economic reform (they claimed, for instance, that old-age pensions would suffer if the opposition took power). The BSP denied seeking a monopoly of power for themselves, and called for the formation of a coalition with the opposition either before or after the elections. Their new image was designed to appeal to Bulgaria's emerging middle class, while in the countryside they conducted a more traditional campaign. In the end, the BSP fell just short of securing a majority of the vote with 47 per cent, but it took over half the seats in parliament and finished well ahead of the UDF opposition. The BSP lost power at further elections in 1991, but it returned in 1994 with 44 per cent of the vote and an overall majority in the parliament.

In Hungary the suppression of the 1956 revolution had been followed by an attempt to develop a national consensus under party leader János Kádár, based upon his formula that 'whoever is not against us is with us' (see Chapter 3). A cautious reform, the New Economic Mechanism, was launched in 1968, and the scope that was available for public debate and for private economic initiative steadily widened. By the 1980s, however, the economy had begun to falter, and there was increasingly open opposition from the cultural intelligentsia and from movements like the Democratic Forum, which was founded in 1987 as a framework for intellectual discussion. The construction of a new dam on the Danube, agreed with the Austrian government in late 1985, had given rise to particular concern among environmentalists. Meanwhile, the regime itself began to experience pressure for change as reformers within its ranks extended the boundaries of permitted debate. Some used the columns of the party press to argue that parliament rather than the party leadership should be the locus of political authority; others were drawn into the preparation of statements that reflected the views of independent economists, such as 'Turnabout and Reform', a call for more far-reaching change that was circulated in late 1986. Another reform manifesto, 'A New Social Contract', appeared the following year, calling directly for political pluralism.

The regime responded in a variety of ways, including personnel change. There was a new prime minister in 1987, Károly Grosz; the following year Grosz took over the party leadership when Kádár and his supporters lost their positions and a young economist, Miklós Németh, became Prime Minister (Kádár died the following year). Action of some kind was clearly necessary if Hungary's rising foreign debt – the largest in the communist world – was to be contained, and it was agreed at a party conference in May 1988 that political as well as economic reform would be required, perhaps even a form of 'socialist pluralism'. But there were divisions within the regime itself in the face of these pressures. Party reformers like Imre Poszgay, a former minister of culture who was rumoured to be Gorbachev's candidate for the leadership, were willing to move towards a Western-style political pluralism with open elections and a choice of party; they were greatly encouraged by the Soviet leader's visit to Hungary in June 1986 and by his close interest in their experience of economic reform, and they were organised in a series of 'reform circles' that operated within party ranks. But others (including Grosz) stood for no more than a modified party ascendancy, although they were willing to accept publicly that the leadership had no 'monopoly of wisdom to solve Hungary's problems'. It would be 'decades', Grosz told *Le Monde* in November 1988, before Hungary could consider a move to multi-party democracy.

The decisive change took place, as elsewhere, during 1989. In January, taking advantage of Grosz's temporary absence in Switzerland, Poszgay used a radio interview to make public the conclusions of a Central Committee commission on the post-war history of Hungary, which described the events of 1956 as a 'popular uprising against an oligarchic system of power that had humiliated the nation' and went on to categorise the 'socialist model' adopted in 1948–9 as 'wrong in its entirety'. In February, following a Central Committee meeting, the party authorities announced that they would be introducing a new constitution in which the party would no longer have a guaranteed monopoly of power, and that they would be prepared to share power in a coalition government. In May party reformers went further, drastically cutting back the *nomenklatura* system of control over appointments, dissolving the party militia and calling for a dialogue with other political forces. In mid-September, after three months of round-table negotiations, the party leadership agreed to hold fresh presidential and parliamentary elections and also approved a new electoral law and depoliticisation of the armed forces. In October, finally, a party congress was held at which a majority of delegates agreed to form a European-style Hungarian Socialist Party, committed to democratic socialism and a mixed economy; a minority of hard-liners, including Grosz, managed to preserve the formal existence of a Hungarian Socialist Workers' Party based on orthodox Marxist principles. Hungary, meanwhile, became a 'republic' once again and not the 'people's republic' it had been since 1949.

Among the many new parties that emerged in these new circumstances, several were of particular significance. One was the Hungarian Democratic Forum, which stood for an amalgam of populist, Christian and nationalist values and the uniquely Hungarian 'third way' that combined political pluralism, support for the traditional family and the defence of Hungarian interests, including Hungarian minorities abroad, tinged in some cases with anti-Semitism. An Alliance of Free Democrats was the successor to the intellectual opposition that had emerged in the 1970s: it stood for a more Western but also a more socially oriented form of liberal democracy than the nationalist HDF, and had more support in the towns than in the countryside. Both held their first national congresses in March 1989. An Alliance of Young Democrats (FIDESz), meanwhile, had been established a year earlier with a broadly social democratic orientation, and with a youthful membership (it was limited to those aged under 35). Party reformers had hoped there would be a presidential election in early 1990, before the parliamentary election that was due later in the year and before oppositional parties could develop their strength; but this proposal was defeated by a narrow margin at a referendum in November 1989, which showed that the HSP was not invincible. By the time the election was called in the spring of 1990 more than eighty other parties had come into existence, of which forty-eight were intending to nominate candidates.

The election took place in two rounds, in March and April 1990. The Democratic Forum was the clear winner, with 42.5 per cent of the vote on a turnout of about 65 per cent. The Alliance of Free Democrats came second with 23.8 per cent and the Independent Smallholders, also anti-communist, were third with 11.4 per cent. The former communists, campaigning as the Hungarian Socialist Party, had to be content with fourth place and just 8.6 per cent of the vote. A coalition government was formed under József Antall, a medical historian and leader of the Hungarian Democratic Forum whose father, a Smallholder, had served in the post-war government. The presidency went to Árpád Göncz, a writer and Free Democrat who had spent six years in prison for his part in the 1956 revolution; and, with some hesitation, the new government embarked upon the path of market and political reform that had been marked out elsewhere in Eastern Europe. There had been virtually no nationwide strikes or anti-government demonstrations, and no loss of life. Instead of this a 'gigantic negotiating machinery' came into operation, involving at least a thousand meetings or discussions and at least as many that were less formally constituted. Not surprisingly, it became known as a 'negotiated revolution'.

THE TRANSITION IN THE USSR

The most fundamental change of all took place in what was still the USSR: fundamental in that it was the largest and most powerful of the communist-ruled countries, and in that it defined the parameters within which the East European states could operate. The USSR had used its military might to crush the Hungarian revolution of 1956, and led its Warsaw Treaty allies into Czechoslovakia to suppress the Prague Spring in 1968. But under Gorbachev the Brezhnev Doctrine was replaced by what his press spokesman jokingly labelled the 'Sinatra Doctrine', under which the states of Eastern Europe were free to do it 'their way'. The Soviet leadership at this time, indeed, not simply permitted but sometimes instigated political reform in Eastern Europe of a kind that was greater than local leaderships were prepared to contemplate. The extent to which they directly intervened in the process of change is still unclear, but they certainly encouraged the opposition to Todor Zhivkov and Erich Honecker, and the student demonstrations that swept Jakes from power in Czechoslovakia. Gorbachev's own view was that 'miscalculations by the ruling parties' had been the main reason for their difficulties, and he was clearly sympathetic to local party reformers who were more in line with his own approach to the kinds of issues they all confronted.

There had been little indication that changes of this kind were likely in March 1985 when a stocky Politburo member from the south of Russia became general secretary of what was still a united and ruling party. Gorbachev, according to his wife at least, had not expected the nomination and spent some time deciding whether to accept it. All that was clear was (in a phrase that later became famous) 'We can't go on like this'. Gorbachev told a Politburo meeting that agreed to nominate him that there was 'no need to change our policies', and there was little public evidence of his longer-term objectives, or even of his personal background. He had not addressed a party congress, had no published collection of writings to his name, and had made only a couple of high-profile visits to foreign countries, to Canada and the United Kingdom, as head of a parliamentary delegation. Only a few important speeches – in particular an address to an ideology conference in December 1984 and an electoral address in February 1985, which mentioned glasnost, social justice and participation – gave some indication of his priorities.

Of all the policies that were promoted by the Gorbachev leadership, glasnost was probably the most distinctive. Glasnost, usually translated as 'openness' or 'publicity', did not mean an unqualified freedom of the press or the right to information, nor was it an original invention of Gorbachev's. It did, however, reflect the new general secretary's belief that without a greater awareness of the real state of affairs and of the considerations that had led to particular decisions there would be no willingness on the part of the Soviet people to commit themselves to his programme of reconstruction or perestroika. 'The better people are informed', Gorbachev told the Central Committee meeting that elected him, 'the more consciously they act, the more actively they support the party, its plans and programmatic objectives.' This led to a more open treatment of social problems such as drugs, prostitution and crime; it also led to a more honest consideration of the Soviet past, including the 'wanton repressive measures' of the 1930s (as Gorbachev put it in a speech of the anniversary of the revolution in 1987), and to an attempt to root out the corruption that had become established during the Brezhnev years.

The 'democratisation' of Soviet political life, of which glasnost was a part, was also intended to release the political energies that, for Gorbachev, had been choked off by the bureaucratic centralisation that developed during the Stalin years. The political system established by the October revolution, he told the 19th Party Conference in 1988, had undergone 'serious deformations', leading to the development of a 'command-administrative system' that had extinguished the democratic potential of the elected soviets. The role of the bureaucratic apparatus had increased out of all proportion, with more than 100 central ministries and 800 in the republics. And it was this 'ossified system of government, with its command-and-pressure mechanism', that had become the main obstacle to change. The Party Conference duly adopted a resolution on 'radical reform' of the political system that provided for a choice of candidate in elections to the soviets, with secret and competitive elections to their executive committees for a maximum of two consecutive terms. There would also be a working parliament for the first time in Soviet history; and all of this would be sustained by a 'rule of law state', within which the rights of ordinary citizens would be securely protected.

Together with these changes, for Gorbachev, there had to be a 'radical reform' of the Soviet economy and an attempt to reverse a decline in the rate of economic growth that had been worsening since the 1950s. In the late 1970s, in the view of Soviet as well as Western commentators, economic growth had probably fallen to zero. Indeed, as Gorbachev explained in early 1988, if the sale of alcoholic drink and of Soviet oil on world markets were excluded, there had been no real growth in the Soviet economy for at least the previous fifteen years. Radical reform, as Gorbachev explained to the 27th Party Congress in 1986 and to a Central Committee meeting the following year, involved a set of related measures. One of the most important was a greater degree of independence for factory workers, allowing them to be guided much more by 'market' indicators than by directives from the central planners, Retail and wholesale prices would gradually be adjusted to reflect the cost of production, and enterprises that persistently failed to pay their way were likely to be dissolved. Farming would increasingly be devolved to family units, there would be a greater diversity of forms of property, and there would be a closer relationship between the Soviet and the international economy, including a fully convertible rouble.

Ultimately this 'third way' that would combine these more democratic forms with a high degree of social equality proved impossible to realise. More open elections, in 1989 and 1990, led not to the return of committed reformers but to the success of nationalist movements in several of the republics, and to the triumph of Boris Yeltsin in the Russian presidential elections of 1991 (Gorbachev himself was elected president by the Soviet parliament in the spring of 1990 and never enjoyed the authority that a popular mandate would have conferred upon him). The opportunity to organise outside the framework of the CPSU led to 'informal' movements and then to political parties that were openly hostile to the CPSU and to socialism. There were demonstrations on an enormous scale, not in support of the 'humane and democratic socialism' to which the party was now committed but (in early 1990) for the removal of its political monopoly from the constitution. Writers and academics, taking advantage of the greater scope that glasnost made available to them, moved towards an explicit critique of Lenin as the founder of a 'totalitarian' system and on to a more general attack on revolutions as the progenitors of violence and repression (see Chapter 8).

Perhaps the most serious failure of all was in the economy, where the old structures of planning were dismantled before any effective market mechanisms had been established to replace them. Economic growth sustained itself for two or three years, but the economy contracted by 4 per cent in 1990 and then by a massive 15 per cent in 1991 as the state itself collapsed. Greater autonomy for enterprises meant, at least in the short term, that they could put up prices more easily, reduce their workforces and eliminate less profitable forms of output. One consequence was serious shortages, including soap and washing powder. 'What kind of a regime is it if we can't even get washed?' asked an indignant group of workers from the Vladimir region. A Moscow housewife threatened to send her washing directly to the ministry concerned: 'If they can't provide us with soap let them do the washing themselves', she reasoned. Another consequence was a significant increase in poverty, as prices raced ahead of earnings and especially pensions; the budgetary deficit widened; and open unemployment emerged for the first time since the end of the 1920s. Gorbachev, his spokesman told the press, had won the Nobel Prize for Peace but not for Economics; anyone who read the plan results for these years would have understood why.

The decisive moment in the collapse of communist rule in the USSR was almost certainly the attempted coup that took place in August 1991. Gorbachev was placed under house arrest at his summer residence in the Crimea when he refused to declare a state of emergency, and in the early hours of 19 August a self-styled 'state emergency committee' announced that he was 'unwell' and that his powers as Soviet president were being assumed by vice-president Yanaev. The Soviet people, warned the conspirators, were in 'mortal danger'. The country had become 'ungovernable'. The economy was in crisis, with a 'chaotic, unregulated slide towards a market', and crime and immorality were rampant. But the coup was resisted from the outset by Boris Yeltsin, who made a dramatic appeal for resistance from a tank in front of the Russian parliament building. And the following night an estimated 70,000 Muscovites surrounded the building in spite of a curfew and protected it against an expected attack. The next day the coup began to collapse – two of the leaders, it emerged, had been drunk for most of its duration – and by the day after the conspirators had been arrested and Gorbachev had been released.

The coup had not been launched by the Communist Party, but the party leadership did little to resist it and the collapse of the attempted coup allowed Boris Yeltsin to order its dissolution. On 23 August, in the Russian parliament, he signed a decree suspending the CPSU throughout the Russian Federation; in November he ordered it banned entirely and seized its property. The Soviet Union was a still greater casualty of the coup. Launched to block the signature of a treaty that would have reconstituted the USSR as a loose confederation, the coup led directly to a series of declarations of independence by the republics and to their assumption of full national sovereignty. The three Baltic republics left in September 1991. And after Ukraine had voted overwhelmingly for full independence in a referendum in early December, the three Slavic republics signed a declaration that established a new Commonwealth of Independent States, withdrawing at the same time from the treaty of union of 1922 that had established the USSR. Most of the other republics joined the CIS shortly afterwards, and Boris Yeltsin moved into Gorbachev's office in the Kremlin when the Soviet president resigned on 25 December. The post-Soviet era had begun.

8　Explaining communist collapse

The collapse, when it came, was sudden and (for almost everyone who studied the region) unexpected. In June 1989 Solidarity won the Polish elections and Eastern Europe acquired its first post-communist administration for forty years; but there was still a communist president, and the new Solidarity government made it clear that Poland's international alliances would be respected. In October Gorbachev was in East Berlin to celebrate the fortieth anniversary of the GDR; in November Nicolae Ceauşescu was re-elected party leader at a 'Congress of the Great Socialist Victory' in Romania. But the breaching of the Berlin Wall on 9 November was a moment of deep symbolism for Europe; the GDR itself collapsed within weeks, and by the end of the year almost all the communist leaders in the region had lost power or even their liberty (Ceauşescu and his wife had lost their lives). The collapse of the USSR followed in 1991, together with the Warsaw Pact and Comecon.

A decade after these momentous events, historians were still arguing about their causes and significance. Were long-term factors, like modernisation and social change, more important than short-term factors, such as the choices that had been made by communist leaderships? To what extent were external or exogenous factors involved – such as the influence of television, or Western diplomacy, or the pressure of the arms race upon smaller and less competitive economies, or what could loosely be called globalisation? And what, indeed, had really changed? The GDR had disappeared entirely, and three of the communist federations – the USSR, Yugoslavia and later Czechoslovakia – had dissolved into their constituent republics. But if there had been a 'transition', it was less clear that it had been a 'transition to democracy': former communist parties were still influential, property had been privatised but allowed to accumulate in the hands of a small group of oligarchs, and although there were elections, there had been only a partial move across the region to a form of limited and accountable government that was based upon the rule of law.

In one of the most extravagant formulations, it was claimed that Eastern Europe had seen not just the end of communist rule, but the 'end of history' itself, as democracy became (in another celebrated phrase) the 'only game in town'. But for others it was more like a recapitulation of the experience of Latin America, where many of the forms of liberal democracy, including competitive elections, were outwardly observed, but where parliaments were weak, drug barons were in government and not in prison, armies were more important actors than political parties, and the poverty of ordinary people coexisted with the ostentatious wealth of a small minority. A simple judgement across an entire continent, of course, was hardly adequate. In Eastern Europe, certainly, there was more evidence of democracy and not just of post-communism in the west of the region – in the Czech Republic and Poland – than in the former Soviet republics, or in the Balkans. In parts of Central Asia, such as Turkmenistan, there had been a reversion to almost medieval forms of personalist dictatorship.

All of this was a reminder of the importance of much older patterns. The countries of 'Western Eastern Europe' (Poland, Hungary, the Czech Republic, Slovakia, Slovenia and the Baltics) had institutions that had developed from Roman law and feudalism, with its balance of rights and obligations. A balance of rights and obligations led naturally to courts of law within which disputes could be regulated, and to parliaments in which the social estates could assert and reconcile their various interests. The countries of western Eastern Europe, moreover, had experienced the Reformation and Counter-Reformation, and their religions placed a premium upon the individual conscience, rather than subordination. Broadly, they had been part of the Austro-Hungarian, not the Russian, empire. And they had experienced genuine elections before the First World War, based on competing political parties and reported by a relatively open press. It was hardly a coincidence that it was the countries of western Eastern Europe, rather later, that allowed a peaceful change of regime through the ballot box, while (at the other extreme) the countries of Central Asia were holding referenda to extend the remits of their already overpowerful presidencies.

The countries of western Eastern Europe, of course, had hardly chosen communist rule in the first place; it had been imposed upon them in the context of the post-war division of the European continent among the major powers. The crucial change was less the product of domestic factors and rather more the decision by the Gorbachev leadership to abandon the Brezhnev Doctrine and allow the countries of the region the opportunity to determine their own destinies. Soviet leaders clearly hoped that reform communists on the model of Gorbachev himself would come to power in place of elderly and incompetent Stalinists, renewing a system that in their view was fundamentally sound. They were even prepared to nudge history in that direction. But if events took a different turn, as they did, the Gorbachev leadership was prepared to accept them in a way its predecessors had been unwilling to contemplate. This meant that changes within the USSR itself were decisive, not just for its own future but for that of the entire region. In this final chapter, accordingly, we consider the collapse of communism primarily in terms of its collapse in the country in which communists had first come to power, and by which its international presence was sustained.

RIVAL EXPLANATIONS OF COMMUNIST COLLAPSE

There had been predictions of the collapse of the Soviet system almost since its establishment. 'No sane man would give them as much as a month to live,' the London-based *Daily Telegraph* declared in January 1918. By November 1919, according to a celebrated contemporary analysis, the *New York Times* had several times reported Lenin killed, imprisoned, planning to flee or living abroad; the government he headed had been pronounced at an end, during its first two years of existence, no fewer than ninety-one times. Later still Andrei Amalrik, one of the first dissidents, asked if the USSR could survive until 1984; the Polish-American scholar Zbigniew Brzezinski wrote of the inevitable collapse of communist regimes more generally in his *Grand Failure*, completed in late 1988.

It was still a surprise, to scholars as much as to the mass public, when the CPSU was banned, Gorbachev resigned and the USSR itself ceased to exist at the end of 1991. The Soviet Union, after all, was an 'indigenous' regime, not one that had been imported in the 'baggage train of the Red Army'. It had developed – apparently – into one of the world's two superpowers. Its government, dissidents themselves agreed, enjoyed substantial popular support even though there were no competitive elections through which that support could readily be demonstrated. For many, especially those inclined to take the longer view, the Soviet regime with all its faults was an organic development out of an authoritarian pre-revolutionary past, and its government rested on something more substantial than coercion. Indeed, when the first largely competitive national elections were held in 1989, communist candidates won over 87 per cent of the seats; and when the USSR itself was put to the vote in the spring of 1991, more than three-quarters of those who took part declared in favour of its continuation as a 'renewed federation'.

What, indeed, had collapsed? Most of the political leaders in the early post-communist years were the same as those who had held sway when the CPSU was the single ruling party: Yeltsin himself in Russia, Aliev in Azerbaijan, Nazarbaev in Kazakhstan, Karimov in Uzbekistan, Shevardnadze in Georgia, Lucinschi in Moldova Leonid Kravchuk, in the Ukraine, had been a less prominent member of the local party leadership; so had his successor, Leonid Kuchma. At local level, at least in post-communist Russia, more than two-thirds of those in administrative office were former party officials. The Communist Party itself was revived in 1993, and soon became the political force with the largest following; its candidates won more seats and votes than any other in the 1995 and 1999 Duma elections, and it had the largest individual membership. The population as a whole, meanwhile, told interviewers that they regretted the demise of the USSR, that they would have been happier if everything had remained as it was in 1985, and that freedom of speech was a welcome change but that multi-party elections were, on the whole, to be regretted.

At least three explanations have been advanced for what was clearly a change of regime, if less clearly a change of system. The first of these focused on ideology. The USSR, it was argued, was an 'ideocratic' state. The authority of its government depended, in this view, upon the political theory of Marxism–Leninism, to which there could be no legitimate challenge. The constitution itself defined the 'highest aim' of the Soviet state as the construction of a 'classless communist society'. The ideology extended to all spheres of public life; it informed the educational system, defined the view that was taken of organised religion and public property, and ruled out alternative ideas, or a market economy, or competing political parties. The ideology, in turn, seemed to be vindicated by the USSR's social progress, by its growing international authority, and by the movement towards some form of socialist rule in the post-colonial countries of Asia and Africa.

The official ideology was certainly in some disarray by the start of the 1990s. Gorbachev had sought to replace a Stalinist socialism with one that was 'humane and democratic'. What was wrong with the old system, he asked the 19th Party Conference in 1988? It was unduly 'statified', leaving no room for citizen initiative. It was heavily bureaucratic, with one in seven employed by the state itself. It was based exclusively upon public ownership and control, with a bias towards defence and heavy industry. And it was monolithic, leaving no room for individual judgement on matters of philosophy or public policy, or for what Gorbachev came eventually to define as political pluralism. Others, mostly party intellectuals, went even further, arguing that there was no alternative to a variety of forms of ownership if civil liberties were to be properly protected, and that Marx and Lenin must bear at least a share of the blame for the political repression and mismanagement that had taken place in a system that claimed to base itself upon their ideas.

As the Soviet crisis deepened, the intellectual critique became sharper still. Marxism, for scholars like Alexander Tsipko, led straight to the Gulag. It was from Marx, Tsipko argued, that Stalin had taken the idea of collectivising small-scale peasant agriculture; and his hostility to the market was not very different from that of other Marxists, nor indeed from the thinking of Marx, Engels and Lenin themselves. It was pointless, from his perspective, to pretend there could be firm guarantees of democracy if all were employed by the state, or of liberty if it was believed that the revolution was its 'own justification and its own law'. Another scholar, the sociologist Igor Klyamkin, argued similarly in early 1989 that Stalinism was not the aberration of a single man but the logical result of Lenin's single-party system, which prized unity more than democracy and had remained largely intact ever since its establishment. Others still went back to the revolution itself, arguing that all changes of this kind were disruptions of a more organic pattern of development and that they led almost inevitably to violence.

Had the collapse of Marxism–Leninism, then, exposed the system to its inevitable demise, if it was not to resort to mass coercion? This was much less clear. For a start, the opinion polls, at the time and later, showed substantial support for the October revolution (43 per cent told interviewers in the early 1990s that they would have supported the Bolsheviks a second time round, with only 6 per cent against), and even for the principles of socialism (67 per cent 'largely' or 'entirely' agreed with the view that socialism 'had its advantages', with only 10 per cent opposed). There had been some support originally for the free market, but it had evaporated by the end of the decade; and Russians were the most likely of all those who were asked in the post-communist countries to think their country was going in the 'wrong direction' (broadly, they thought they had lived best under Leonid Brezhnev). Russians, it seemed, wanted a 'socialism that worked', with full employment and low prices, but in which their individual liberties were also respected. And where Marxism–Leninism was rejected, it was less often for capitalism than for a kind of 'third way' that respected Russia's special traditions and circumstances.

It was far from clear, in any case, that beliefs of this or any kind mattered for the survival of the regime. The Soviet government had been established in the first place on the basis of 'bread, peace and land', not theoretical abstractions. It had led its people to victory in the Second World War, with communists in the front line; and it had guaranteed their employment, housing, health care and education. If living standards had still been improving in the late 1980s, would it have mattered very much if the philosophical assumptions of the founders of the Soviet system had been thought a little unsatisfactory? Was it 'socialism' that had been rejected, or a form of authoritarianism that used the same language? And even if there was some popular discontent, did it necessarily prejudice the survival of a regime that did not depend – until it chose to introduce them – upon its success at competitive elections?

Clearer, perhaps, was the impact of national and ethnic self-assertion. The old Soviet system had in theory provided for all legitimate needs of this kind

through a complex federal structure and an extensive range of constitu-
tionally guaranteed freedoms. Nominally, at least, each of the fifteen Soviet
republics was a member of a 'voluntary' union with the right to secede at any
time. Each had its own government and parliament, and most of the functions
of state were shared with Moscow or devolved entirely (defence and foreign
affairs, together with the most important economic ministries, were under
central control but accountable to the all-union parliament). Russian was
the language of inter-republic communication, but local languages had
an equivalent status in each of the republics. Any kind of racial or national
discrimination was illegal under the constitution, and with an increasing
proportion of ethnically mixed marriages and a greater knowledge of Russian
it appeared that the Soviet system had effectively combined national diversity
– there were up to 800 distinct communities, with Russians just over half the
total – with a working balance between central and local authority.

The Brezhnev leadership, in the 1970s, began to call the Soviet peoples
a 'new historical community' whose separate identities would eventually
disappear; and Gorbachev, in his earliest speeches, took a very similar
position. Addressing the 26th Congress of the CPSU in 1986, he spoke of
Soviet nationalities policy as an 'outstanding achievement of socialism' that
had 'done away for ever' with national oppression and inequalities of all kinds.
An 'indissoluble friendship' among the Soviet nations had been established
and a Soviet people had come into being, a 'qualitatively new social and inter-
ethnic community cemented by the same economic interests, ideology and
political goals'. Gorbachev had to acknowledge, however, that there could be
'contradictions' among these fraternal nations, and as his leadership advanced
these reservations became an increasingly prominent feature of his addresses.
By 1987, after riots had taken place in Kazakhstan, he had begun to argue for
the need for adequate representation of the various nationalities in political and
economic life, and to complain about the superficial way in which such matters
had been discussed by the scholarly community. Eventually, in September
1989, a long-promised Central Committee plenary meeting on the national
question was held, which agreed with Gorbachev that a 'renewed federation'
was needed with greater rights for the republics (including Russia) but under
the 'consolidating and directing' control of the CPSU.

The national question was one that, in retrospect, the Soviet leader agreed
he had been too slow to address, and it was certainly true that policy changes
tended to follow rather than shape events. There were, broadly speaking,
two different sets of issues. In the first place, there were 'communal' tensions
between national groups within as much as between the Soviet republics.
These differences began to emerge in Nagorno-Karabakh, an autonomous
republic largely populated by Christian Armenians that had formed part
of Muslim Azerbaijan since 1923. In February 1988, in an historic vote,

the Nagorno-Karabakh parliament agreed to request a change of status, from Azerbaijani to Armenian control. This open gesture of defiance led to massive demonstrations of support in Armenia, but to pogroms and angry resistance in Azerbaijan, and eventually to the outbreak of a military conflict between the two republics combined with a form of 'ethnic cleansing' in each of them. At least 300,000 became refugees, and there were thousands of casualties.

The other disputes that emerged in the late 1980s were more 'traditional' in character, taking the form (for the most part) of movements for national self-determination. The clearest case was in the Baltic, whose three republics had been incorporated into the USSR as late as 1940 following a coerced vote by their respective parliaments. The first large-scale demonstrations erupted in August 1987, on the anniversary of the Nazi–Soviet pact that had led to the republics' incorporation into the USSR (the pact and its secret protocols were not acknowledged in official sources at this time). Baltic discontent was the result of several factors. One of them was the very real concern that, with low birth rates and high levels of immigration, the Baltic nationals (especially the Latvians and Estonians) might become minorities in their own republics. And there was concern about the environmental damage the republics had suffered as a result of decisions taken in Moscow. Influenced by such concerns, the republican leaderships began to call for a greater degree of local autonomy, and 'national fronts' developed which, in 1990, swept the board at elections to the local parliaments. Lithuania at once declared independence on the basis of its prewar constitution; the other two republics committed themselves to a more gradual change of status. Independence was supported by large majorities in republican referenda in the spring of 1991; the following September, after the coup had collapsed, all three republics were granted their wishes and admitted into the United Nations as fully sovereign states.

The 'national question', certainly, led directly to the collapse of the USSR as a centralised state with fifteen union republics. And yet here again hindsight can mislead. There were several 'national questions', not just one, and only in the Baltic (and perhaps Transcaucasia) did the local national question take the form of a demand for immediate independence. Did the USSR, as a concept, command popular support? The evidence of the referendum of March 1991 was that it did, although the wording of the question was too complicated to allow a simple conclusion to be drawn. On a turnout of 80 per cent, 76 per cent declared in favour of the USSR as a 'renewed federation of equal sovereign republics in which the human rights and freedoms of every nationality [would] be fully guaranteed': a mandate, Gorbachev claimed, for the 'renewal and strengthening of the union'. Discussions continued on the elaboration of a treaty that would redefine the rights of the USSR and of its constituent republics, and in November 1991 nine of the original fifteen agreed on a new 'union of sovereign states'.

It was a referendum in the Ukraine on 1 December that precipitated the final break-up. Ukrainians voted solidly for independence (these were the same Ukrainians who had voted solidly for a reformed USSR in the spring); the Yeltsin government refused to enter a new union without them; and on 8 December the Russian, Ukrainian and Belorussian leaders established the Commonwealth of Independent States, a new grouping that was based on the full independence of each of its members. With a network of CIS institutions, an initial commitment to the rouble zone and to a military defence pact that extended to most of its members, there were indeed some grounds for considering the CIS a continuation of the USSR (minus the Baltics) in something like the 'renewed' form that Gorbachev had originally envisaged. And it was equally clear that national differences, handled skilfully and in more favourable economic circumstances, might have found expression within a reformed USSR and not necessarily outside it.

Was it, then, the economic factor that ultimately had led to the collapse of Soviet rule? There was certainly no doubt, as we saw in Chapter 7, that Soviet economic performance had steadily dropped below the historic levels of the years of industrialisation. Gorbachev's answer was a shift from 'extensive' to 'intensive' growth, with greater independence for enterprises, a variety of forms of property, prices that reflected relative scarcities, and greater rights for ordinary workers at their place of employment so that the 'human factor' could reassert itself. The twelfth Five-Year Plan, adopted on this basis in 1986, called for a doubling of national income by the year 2000. A series of legislative measures spelled out these objectives in more detail: in November 1986 a range of private economic activities (including car repairs and photography) was legalised; and in 1987 a law on the state enterprise sought to bring 'real economic independence' to the factories that were responsible for fulfilling output targets. In 1988 a further law encouraged the development of cooperatives, which were to function outside the system of state planning and could (in principle) set their own prices. And in 1989 legislation on agriculture sought to facilitate a transition from state or cooperative farms to small and more cost-effective family units.

If the central objective of these reforms was to raise the rate of economic growth and to improve living standards in particular, it was clear by the late 1980s that they had failed to do so. The rate of economic growth up to 1989 averaged 3.7 per cent, exactly the same as the figure for the late Brezhnev and Andropov years. In 1990 national income fell, according to official sources, and in 1991 the extreme fall of about 15 per cent was greater in relative terms than that which the USA had experienced during the collapse of the 1930s. Some contribution was made by a change in the terms of trade, and by disasters such as the Chernobyl explosion of April 1986 and the Armenian earthquake of December 1988. Many of the reforms, in any case, remained largely on paper. And yet the results, as ordinary people experienced them in the late 1980s and early 1990s, were clearly of a kind that might call into question the 'social contract' on which, it was widely agreed, the stability of the Soviet system had been based.

The collapse of economic performance in the late Gorbachev years had a wide range of effects on ordinary people, if the contemporary press was any guide. As money incomes rose but output fell, shortages became worse; soap, matches, washing powder, salt and other basic commodities were all affected, and sugar disappeared for reasons that were also connected with the anti-alcohol campaign. Not only were shortages getting worse, so was quality. The weekly paper *Literaturnaya gazeta*, in an experiment, tried out some sausage on thirty cats who 'knew nothing of chemistry, bureaucracy or economies of scale'. In the event, twenty-four refused all of the varieties they were offered, and five more refused most of them. Queues became longer and prices rose sharply as producers took advantage of their greater opportunity to profit from circumstances of acute shortage. The black market boomed, enriching a criminal underground. At the other end of the spectrum up to a quarter of the population was living below the poverty line by 1990, with large families, pensioners and an increasing number of unemployed among the worst affected.

Was this, then, the decisive factor in the end of seventy years or more of Soviet rule? Again it seems wisest to avoid deterministic conclusions. Yeltsin's government, in 1992 and 1993, presided over a collapse in economic output that was even steeper, and yet it managed to survive; indeed, its social and economic policies were supported by a majority of those who voted in a referendum in the spring of 1993. Governments elsewhere have sustained a fall in their economic performance, including Western Europe in the early 1980s. A substantial literature on revolutions and political change has generally emphasised perceptions at least as much as economic performance itself. In pre-revolutionary France, it has been pointed out, living standards were steadily rising; what was crucial was their failure to continue to do so, as compared with the expectation that they would, in 1788 and 1789. From this point of view it was the failure to sustain expectations at the end of the 1980s, not the fall of national income itself, that precipitated political change.

It was clear, after a steady and apparently systemic fall in rates of growth, that the Soviet economic system would require a fundamental reconsideration. China, however, showed that an economy could be liberalised – and apparently with great success – while the political forms of communist rule were retained. And even if there was a need for fundamental reform, we still need to explain why it came when it did and took the form that it did.

Communist rule in the USSR, after all, collapsed; it was not overthrown. It was very different in the Baltics, where there were huge public demonstrations against communist rule and sweeping successes for nationalists at the polls. It was different from Czechoslovakia, where half the population had taken part in a general strike in favour of the end of communist rule in late November 1989; and different from Poland, where Solidarity had secured an overwhelming majority of the freely contested seats in the elections of June 1989. There was no obvious moment at which the Soviet peoples, or at least the Russian majority, had clearly chosen a post-communist future.

'Men make their own history', Marx had remarked; 'but they do not make it as they choose.' So an adequate understanding of the end of the system he had foretold must bring together 'structure' (the wider context of communist rule) and 'agency' (the people whose choices made a difference at decisive moments). It was unlikely that communist rule would survive without modifications; but that left open several options, including a 'Chinese' combination of market reform and political authoritarianism, and the kind of 'third way' that Gorbachev was seeking, in which a wide range of political forces would combine under the guidance of a reformed communist party within a system that guaranteed the basic liberties of all of its citizens. In the end the pattern of events in the late 1980s and early 1990s owed much to other, much shorter-range considerations, and to those directly involved. In particular, the pattern of events owed much to the power struggle between Gorbachev and Boris Yeltsin, a struggle in which Yeltsin was able to use the hostility that had developed towards the party bureaucracy to his own advantage through the electoral process that had opened up in the late 1980s. Yeltsin, at this time, was opposed to a communist monopoly of power, but not necessarily to a political system in which they would retain the dominant influence. And he had certainly no deliberate intention of dissolving the USSR; he was so drunk during the negotiations that led to the formation of the Commonwealth of Independent States that he fell off his chair, and it was later a development he bitterly regretted.

It was even less clear, more than ten years after the end of communist rule, what had replaced it. On the face of it, a great transition had taken place; and certainly there were new governments throughout the region. But many of the changes that we associate with post-communist rule had already taken place in the last years of Soviet government: freedom of the press, freedom of conscience, multi-party politics and private ownership in the economy. Equally, there were strongly 'Soviet' elements in the system that developed after 1991; indeed, there were still longer-term continuities, in that the Soviet system had itself incorporated many of the 'Russian' features of the system that had existed up to 1917. How, Chou En-lai had been asked, would he evaluate the French revolution? It was, thought the great Chinese statesman, 'too soon to say'. A decade after the end of communist rule in Eastern Europe, it would be premature to suggest that it has marked not just a change of regime but a departure from much longer-standing patterns of strong and sometimes authoritarian government balanced by a society with few of the attitudes and practices that helped to sustain democracy elsewhere on the continent.

Further reading

There is a large and increasing literature on the recent history of Central and Eastern Europe, and on communist rule itself. The suggestions that follow are confined to book-length publications in English. There is also an abundant periodical literature, particularly in journals such as *Europe–Asia Studies, East European Politics and Societies, East European Quarterly, Slavic Review, Journal of Communist Studies and Transition Politics*, and *Communist and Post-Communist Studies*. Most of these, in addition to articles, carry reviews of recent publications.

Two *bibliographies* might first of all be mentioned: Raymond E. Pearson, *Russia and Eastern Europe, 1789–1985* (Manchester: Manchester University Press, 1989); and Raymond C. Taras, ed., *A Handbook of Political Science Research on the USSR and Eastern Europe: Trends from the 1950s to the 1990s* (Westport, CT: Greenwood Press, 1992).

There are several good *historical atlases*, including Richard J. Crampton and Ben Crampton, *Atlas of Eastern Europe in the Twentieth Century* (London: Routledge, 1996); Dennis P. Hupchick and Harold E. Cox, *A Concise Historical Atlas of Eastern Europe* (New York: St Martin's, 1996); and Paul Robert Magocsi, *A Historical Atlas of East Central Europe* (Seattle: University of Washington Press, 1995).

Data covering a wide range of topics over extended periods of time may be consulted in a variety of international publications, but also in B. P. Pockney, *Soviet Statistics since 1950* (Aldershot: Dartmouth, 1991); and Paul S. Shoup, *The East European and Soviet Data Handbook: Political, Social, and Developmental Indicators 1945–1975* (New York: Columbia University Press, 1981).

Among collections of documents, the following may be noted: Stephen Clissold, ed., *Yugoslavia and the Soviet Union 1939–1973: A Documentary Survey* (London: Oxford University Press/RIIA, 1975); Alexander Dallin, ed., *Diversity in International Communism: A Documentary Record, 1961–1963* (New York and London: Columbia University Press, 1963); Robert V. Daniels, ed., *A Documentary History of Communism*, 2 vols (London: Tauris, 1985); Russian Institute, Columbia University, *The Anti-Stalin Campaign and International Communism* (New York: Columbia University Press, 1956); Gale Stokes, ed., *From Stalinism to Pluralism: A Documentary History of Eastern Europe since 1945*, 2nd edn (New York: Oxford University Press, 1996); Bogdan Szajkowski, ed., *Documents in Communist Affairs 1981* (London: Butterworths, 1981; other volumes are available); and Paul E. Zinner, ed., *National Communism and Popular Revolt in Eastern Europe* (New York: Columbia University Press, 1956).

Reference works that relate to the area include: Stephen White, ed., *Handbook of Reconstruction in Eastern Europe and the Soviet Union* (Harlow: Longman, 1991); and Stephen White, ed., *Political and Economic Encyclopedia of the Soviet Union and Eastern Europe* (Harlow: Longman, and Chicago: St James Press, 1990). These may be kept up to date by consulting surveys and news digests, such as the *Annual Register, Keesing's Record of World Events* and *Facts on File.*

General histories of the region include: Robert Bideleux and Ian Jeffries, *A History of Eastern Europe: Crisis and Change* (London: Routledge, 1998); Zbigniew K. Brzezinski, *The Soviet Bloc: Unity and Conflict*, 2nd edn (Cambridge, MA: Harvard University Press, 1967); Richard J. Crampton, *Eastern Europe in the Twentieth Century – and after*, 2nd edn (London: Routledge, 1997); Joseph Held, ed., *The Columbia History of Eastern Europe in the Twentieth Century* (New York: Columbia University Press, 1992); Paul G. Lewis, *Central Europe since 1945* (London: Longman, 1994); Joseph Rothschild and Nancy M. Wingfield, *Return to Diversity: A Political History of East Central Europe since World War II*, 3rd edn (New York: Oxford University Press, 2000); and Geoffrey Swain and Nigel Swain, *Eastern Europe since 1945*, 2nd edn (London: Macmillan, 1998).

There are also several *histories of communism*: Fernando Claudin, *The Communist Movement: From Comintern to Cominform* (Harmondsworth: Penguin, 1975); F. W. Deakin *et al.*, *A History of World Communism* (London: Weidenfeld & Nicolson, 1975); Hugh Seton-Watson, *The Pattern of Communist Revolution: A History of World Communism*, 2nd edn (London: Methuen, 1960); Hugh Seton-Watson, *Imperialist Revolutionaries: Trends in World Communism in the 1960s and 1970s* (Stanford, CA: Hoover Institution Press, 1978); and Adam Westoby, *Communism since World War II* (Brighton: Harvester, 1981).

On the *establishment and early history* of communist rule in Eastern Europe, see Francois Fejto, *A History of the People's Democracies: Eastern Europe since Stalin*, rev. edn (Harmondsworth: Penguin, 1974); Thomas T. Hammond, ed., *The Anatomy of Communist Takeovers* (New Haven, CT: Yale University Press, 1975); Martin McCauley, ed., *Communist Power in Europe, 1944–1949* (London: Macmillan, 1977); and Norman Naimark and Leonid Gibianskii, eds, *The Establishment of Communist Regimes in Eastern Europe 1944–49* (Boulder, CO: Westview, 1997).

Among historical studies of the *collapse of communist rule* at the end of the 1980s, see J.F. Brown, *Surge to Freedom: The End of Communist Rule in Eastern Europe* (Durham, NC: Duke University Press, 1991); Roger East and Jolyon Ponton, *Revolution and Change in Central and Eastern Europe*, 2nd edn (London: Pinter, 1997); Timothy Garton Ash, *We the People: The Revolution of 1989* (Harmondsworth: Penguin, 1990); David S. Mason, *Revolution and Transition in East-Central Europe*, 2nd edn (Boulder, CO: Westview, 1996); and Gale Stokes, *The Walls Came Tumbling Down: The Collapse of Communism in Eastern Europe* (New York: Oxford University Press, 1993).

Economic developments may be followed through: Ian Jeffries, ed., *Socialist Economies and the Transition to the Market: A Guide* (London: Routledge, 1993); Michael Kaser, ed., *The Economic History of Eastern Europe, 1919–1975*, 3 vols

(Oxford: Oxford University Press, 1985–6); and Marie Lavigne, *The Economics of Transition: From Socialist Economy to Market Economy*, 2nd edn (Basingstoke: Macmillan, 1999). Subsequent developments are best followed through international organisations and their websites: the European Bank for Reconstruction and Development, which publishes a *Transition Report (www.ebrd.com)*; the Organisation for Economic Cooperation and Development *(www.oecd.org)*; the United Nations Economic Commission for Europe, which has for some time published an annual *Economic Survey of Europe (www.unece.org)*; and the World Bank, which publishes an annual *World Development Report (www.worldbank.org)*.

On *changing societies*, see, for instance, Ian Bremmer and Ray Taras, eds, *New States, New Politics: Building the Post-Soviet States* (Cambridge: Cambridge University Press, 1997); Walter D. Connor, *Socialism, Politics, and Equality: Hierarchy and Change in Eastern Europe and the USSR* (New York: Columbia University Press, 1979); Chris Corrin, ed., *Superwomen and the Double Burden: Women's Experience of Change in East-Central Europe and the Former Soviet Union* (London: Scarlet Press, 1992); Milovan Djilas, *The New Class: An Analysis of the Communist System* (London: Thames & Hudson, 1957); Ferenc Fehér, Agnes Heller and György Márkus, *Dictatorship over Needs: An Analysis of Soviet Societies* (Oxford: Blackwell 1983); and David Lane, *The End of Social Inequality? Class, Status and Power under State Socialism* (London: George Allen & Unwin 1982).

There are several surveys or more analytic studies of the *politics of the region*, including William L. Miller, Stephen White and Paul Heywood, *Values and Political Change in Postcommunist Europe* (London: Macmillan, and New York: St Martin's, 1998); Richard Rose, William Mishler and Christian Haerpfer, *Democracy and its Alternatives: Understanding Postcommunist Societies* (Baltimore, MD: Johns Hopkins University Press, 1998); George Schopflin, *Politics in Eastern Europe, 1945–1992* (Oxford: Blackwell, 1993); and Stephen White, Judy Batt and Paul G. Lewis, eds, *Developments in Central and East European Politics 2* (London: Macmillan, 1998).

On *public opinion*, see particularly the *Central and Eastern Eurobarometer* (Brussels: European Commission, since 1991), and the *New Russia Barometer* and *New Democracies Barometer*, organised by the Centre for the Study of Public Policy at the University of Strathclyde, Scotland (for a full listing see www.strath.ac.uk/Departments/CSPP).

Among many studies of *individual countries*, the following may be noted:

The Baltic countries

Rein Taagepera and Romuald Misiunas, *The Baltic States: Years of Dependence 1940–80* (London: Hurst, 1983)

Belarus

David Marples, *Belarus: From Soviet Rule to Nuclear Catastrophe* (London: Macmillan, 1996)

Bulgaria

Richard J. Crampton, *A Short History of Modern Bulgaria* (Cambridge: Cambridge University Press, 1987)

Czechoslovakia

J. F. N. Bradley, *Czechoslovakia's Velvet Revolution: A Political Analysis* (Boulder, CO: East European Monographs, 1992)
Galia Golan, *The Czechoslovak Reform Movement: Communism in Crisis, 1962–1968* (Cambridge: Cambridge University Press, 1971)
Galia Golan, *Reform Rule in Czechoslovakia: the Dubcek Era, 1968–1969* (Cambridge: Cambridge University Press, 1973)
Vladimir Kusin, *The Intellectual Origins of the Prague Spring* (Cambridge: Cambridge University Press, 1971)
Jaromir Navratil, ed., *The Prague Spring, 1968* (Budapest: Central European University Press, 1998)
H. Gordon Skilling, *Czechoslovakia's Interrupted Revolution* (Princeton, NJ: Princeton University Press, 1976)
Bernard Wheaton and Zdenek Kavan, *The Velvet Revolution: Czechoslovakia 1988–1991* (Boulder, CO: Westview, 1992)
Sharon Wolchik, *Czechoslovakia in Transition: Politics, Economics, and Society* (London: Pinter, 1991)

German Democratic Republic

Mary Fulbrook, *Anatomy of a Dictatorship: Inside the GDR 1949–1989* (Oxford: Oxford University Press, 1995)
Charles S. Maier, *Dissolution: The Crisis of Communism and the End of East Germany* (Princeton, NJ: Princeton University Press, 1997)
Martin McCauley, *The German Democratic Republic since 1945* (London: Macmillan, 1983)

Hungary

Terry Cox, ed., *Hungary 1956 – Forty Years On* (London and Portland, OR: Cass, 1997)
Jeno Gyorkei and Miklos Horvath, eds, *Soviet Military Intervention in Hungary 1956* (Budapest: Central European University Press, 1999)
Agnes Horvath and Arpad Szakolczai, *The Dissolution of Communist Power: The Case of Hungary* (London and New York: Routledge, 1992)

Gyorgy Litvan, *The Hungarian Revolution of 1956* (London: Longman, 1996)

Bill Lomax, *Hungary 1956* (London: Allison & Busby, 1976)

Nigel Swain, *Hungary: The Rise and Fall of Feasible Socialism* (London: Verso, 1992)

Rudolf L. Tokes, *Hungary's Negotiated Revolution* (Cambridge: Cambridge University Press, 1996)

Poland

Neil Ascherson, *The Polish August* (Harmondsworth: Penguin, 1981)

Norman Davies, *God's Playground: A History of Poland in Two Volumes* (Oxford: Clarendon Press, 1981)

M. K. Dziewanowski, *Poland in the Twentieth Century* (New York: Columbia University Press, 1977)

Timothy Garton Ash, *The Polish Revolution: Solidarity 1980–82* (London: Cape, 1983)

Bartomoliej Kaminski, *The Collapse of State Socialism: The Case of Poland* (Princeton, NJ: Princeton University Press, 1991)

R. F. Leslie, ed., *The History of Poland since 1863* (Cambridge: Cambridge University Press, 1980)

Kevin Ruane, *The Polish Challenge* (London: BBC, 1982)

George Sanford, *Polish Communism in Crisis* (London: Croom Helm, 1983)

Richard Staar, ed., *The Transition to Democracy in Poland* (New York: St Martin's, 1993)

Jadwiga Staniszkis, *The Dynamics of the Breakthrough in Eastern Europe: The Polish Experience* (Berkeley: University of California Press, 1991)

Romania

Martin Rady, *Romania in Turmoil: A Contemporary History* (London: Tauris, 1992)

Russia/USSR

Archie Brown, *The Gorbachev Factor* (Oxford: Oxford University Press, 1996)

Richard Sakwa, *Gorbachev and his Reforms, 1985–1990* (Hemel Hempstead: Philip Allan, 1990)

Richard Sakwa, *The Rise and Fall of the Soviet Union, 1917–1991* (London: Routledge, 1999)

Stephen White, *After Gorbachev*, 4th rev. edn (Cambridge: Cambridge University Press, 1994)

Ukraine

Taras Kuzio and Andrew Wilson, eds, *Ukraine: Perestroika to Independence* (London: Macmillan, 1992)

Bohdan Nahaylo, *The Ukrainian Resurgence* (London: Hurst, 1999)
Orest Subtely, *Ukraine: A History* (Toronto: University of Toronto Press, 1988)
Andrew Wilson, *Ukrainian Nationalism in the 1990s: A Minority Faith* (Cambridge: Cambridge University Press, 1997)
Andrew Wilson, *The Ukranians: Unexpected Nation* (New Haven, CT, and London: Yale University Press, 2000)

Yugoslavia

Misha Glenny, *The Balkans, 1804–1999* (Cambridge: Granta, 1999)
Tim Judah, *Kosovo* (New Haven, CT, and London: Yale University Press, 2000)
Fred Singleton, *A Short History of the Yugoslav Peoples* (Cambridge: Cambridge University Press, 1985)

Index